SERVING LOVE

THE DIVORCE-PROOFING AMERICA'S MARRIAGES
CAMPAIGN PRESENTS:

SERVING LOVE

BY DR. GARY AND BARBARA ROSBERG

Tyndale House Publishers, Inc.
Wheaton, Illinois

Visit Tyndale's exciting Web site at www.tyndale.com

Serving Love

Copyright © 2003 by Gary and Barbara Rosberg. All rights reserved.

Cover photograph copyright © 2003 by Brian MacDonald. All rights reserved.

Authors' photo copyright © 2002 by Thomas and Bruce Photography. All rights reserved.

Interior illustrations copyright © 2002 by Mona Caron. All rights reserved.

Designed by Julie Chen

Edited by Linda K. Taylor

Produced with the assistance of The Livingstone Corporation (www.LivingstoneCorp.com).

Published in association with the literary agency of Alive Communications, Inc., 7680 Goddard Street, Suite 200, Colorado Springs, CO 80920.

Unless otherwise indicated, all Scripture quotations are taken from the *Holy Bible*, New Living Translation, copyright © 1996. Used by permission of Tyndale House Publishers, Inc., Wheaton, Illinois 60189. All rights reserved.

All quotations are taken from *The Five Love Needs of Men and Women* by Dr. Gary and Barbara Rosberg, published by Tyndale House, 2000.

ISBN 0-8423-7343-8

Printed in the United States of America.

09 08 07 06 05 04 03

7 6 5 4 3 2 1

Dedication

To Linda Taylor

*Thank you for using your passion and gifts
to make this workbook a reality.
Your heart for Tom, the love of your life,
is a wonderful example of what
we pray spreads across the country through the
Divorce-Proofing America's Marriages campaign.*

CONTENTS

A SPECIAL NOTE FROM GARY AND BARB

Dear friends,

We are so glad that you have decided to spend several weeks on learning more about your spouse's needs and how to meet them. We know that your time will reap significant benefits—not only in your own marriage but also in the people on whom your marriage has an impact: your children, your larger family, your friends, your community, and beyond. You may be surprised by that list, but we really believe that the health of our marriages affects lots of people.

When you decided to do this workbook, you became part of a large group of couples across this nation—from Boston to Los Angeles, from Miami to Seattle—who are joining together to divorce-proof their marriages. They are taking a stand *for* healthy, growing, lifetime marriages and *against* the looming threat of divorce.

Most of you will be working through this book in the context of a small group; that's the most effective environment because you benefit from each other's perspectives, encouragement, prayer, and accountability. But even if you are going through the book on your own, we know you and your marriage will be changed.

This book is part of our larger campaign, Divorce-Proofing America's Marriages. The flagship book in that campaign, *Divorce-Proofing Your Marriage,* outlines six loves—forgiving love, serving love, persevering love, guarding love, celebrating love, and renewing love—that will strengthen your marriage and keep you from sliding toward disappointment, discord, and possibly even emotional divorce.

This workbook is a companion to our *The Five Love Needs of Men and Women* book, which addresses the serving love component. If you haven't read *Divorce-Proof Your Marriage* and worked through the companion workbook, *Discover the Love of Your Life All Over Again,* that's all right. But your group may want to do that sometime in the future. (For a list of other campaign products, see the appendix at the back of this book, or log on to our Web site at **www.divorceproof.com.**)

We wish you God's richest blessings as you learn to serve your spouse by learning how to meet his or her needs.

Your friends,
Gary and Barb Rosberg

Introduction

HOW TO USE THIS BOOK
COURSE PURPOSE:
TO LEARN TO UNDERSTAND AND MEET YOUR SPOUSE'S LOVE NEEDS.

This eight-week workbook course by Gary and Barbara Rosberg will help you serve your spouse by learning what his or her top five love needs are and by discovering how to meet those needs. When you do that, you will increase your love for each other and divorce-proof your marriage.

Each person will need his/her own copy of this workbook. Each couple will also need a copy of the book *The Five Love Needs of Men and Women* because the weekly assignments include reading chapters from the book. That book is laid out with an introductory chapter followed by ten chapters—five written by Gary as he talks to wives about their husbands' top five love needs and five written by Barb as she talks to husbands about their wives' top five love needs. As part of your assignments to read the book, both husband and wife should read the two chapters that focus on each love need from both perspectives.

This workbook is designed to equip you to

- identify how you can meet the five love needs of your spouse;
- discover godly attitudes of the heart necessary to meet those needs;
- practice meeting each love need in your spouse; and
- journal your progress on each weekly assignment.

Each week you will meet with your group for some general discussion (don't worry, no baring of your soul or pouring out your heart in front of others). The group discussion is to guide you to think about the topic. Included in the group time are opportunities for just you and your spouse to talk as well.

The heart of the study, however, comes in the homework assignments. After each group lesson you will find three sections for you to work on during the week.

Day One is a time of **Personal Reflection**. Here you will

- Write down how each love need sounds, looks, and feels to you personally. You will be asked what that need looks like to you, sounds like to you, and feels like when the need is met. For your Couple Interaction time (Day Two), your spouse will be asking you to answer this specifically so he/she can discover how to meet that need in your life.
- Determine how you can serve your spouse by meeting that love need.

Day Two is a time for **Couple Interaction.** Here you will

- Take turns sharing how that particular love need being discussed sounds, looks, and feels in each other's lives.
- Discuss with your spouse how you can meet that particular love need.

Day Three is called **My Assignment**, where you will

- Complete a reading assignment of two chapters of *The Five Love Needs of Men and Women* by Gary and Barbara Rosberg.
- Plan and practice meeting your spouse's specific love need during the week.
- Journal your progress by writing down what you did to practice meeting your spouse's need and chronicle his/her response.

Gary and Barb say:

You need to know your spouse's heart and needs, and then sacrificially step away from your own selfishness and learn—really learn—how to meet those needs. You must build your life on a foundation that is going to stand the test of the storms—a rock-solid foundation that will not shift under pressure. . . . Houses don't do well on sandy foundations. Neither do relationships. Marriages built on the rock of Christ Jesus not only start strong but also finish strong.

(page 7)

Group Session One

WHAT ARE YOUR LOVE NEEDS?

SETTING THE MOOD

1. Describe your favorite television or movie couple (from any era). What do you like about the dynamic between those two people?

    _____

    _____

    _____

2. If you can, describe one of your favorite episodes or interchanges between those two people.

    _____

    _____

    _____

Obviously, the couples we see on the big (or small) screen are created for an audience. They read scripts written by writers who are seeking to get you to laugh or cry. Sometimes they seem very true to life; at other times they are not. We are drawn to various characters for various reasons: the romance between Rhett and Scarlett, the intensity between Bogart and Bacall, the humor between Raymond and everybody who loves him (including his wife).

Every marriage has its own dynamic; every husband and wife team is very different because, obviously, the individuals are different. We may long for the type of household we see on the screen, but to build the strongest marriages, we need to build on strong foundations—not on fantasies, but on reality.

So, what is the reality for your marriage? Do you know what your spouse's love needs are?

Don't worry—if you don't know, you're about to find out! That's what this study is all about.

DISCOVERING THE NEED

Gary and Barb say:

Meeting your spouse's love needs is one of the most important responsibilities you have in your marriage. . . . Human nature is strange. Something in us assumes that if we treat our spouse the way we would like him or her to treat us, we are meeting our partner's needs. But when it comes to needs, the Golden Rule does not always apply. Why? Because in many cases a husband's needs are different from a wife's needs. . . . If I asked you if you are meeting your spouse's love needs, you would probably answer yes. In reality, what many of us are really doing is just assuming our spouse wants what we want, and so we act on that. Often we really don't know what our spouse's needs are. And if we don't know what the needs are, we can't possibly meet them effectively.
(pages 5, 8)

3. God created us to need relationships with others and, most important, with him. While we can easily understand that we need certain things to survive physically, what do we need to survive relationally? As a group, identify various love needs you think God created each of us with, and write them below.

   _____

   _____

   _____

4. Read in Genesis 2:18-25 what God (and Adam) said about marriage. What physical and relational needs are to be met in the marriage relationship?

   _____

   _____

   _____

When we wrote our book *The Five Love Needs of Men and Women,* we surveyed more than 700 couples. We gave them a list of twenty needs and asked each spouse to individually rank, in order of importance, what he or she needed from the spouse and what the spouse needed from them. You can look at the list in appendix B.

As you can see from that list, we expect a lot from each other, don't we? You surely have had a need for everything on that list at one time or another. Obviously, it is not realistic to expect your spouse to be able to meet all of those needs for you at all times.

5. Ultimately, to whom should we look for fulfillment of all our needs? (Read Philippians 4:19.) _____

6. At the same time, however, God gave us marriage. To make it the best it can be, we need to be doing our best to meet our spouse's love needs. In what ways do you think that understanding each other's top five love needs could help improve people's marriages?

_____

_____

_____

For the purposes of this book, we will be focusing on the top five love needs that we discovered in our survey. As different as we know men and women are, we found it interesting that the top five love needs for both husbands and wives are almost identical, although men and women ranked them in a slightly different order. In the following chart, number 1 indicates the most important love need.

Husbands' Top Five Love Needs
1. Unconditional Love and Acceptance
2. Sexual Intimacy
3. Companionship
4. Encouragement and Affirmation
5. Spiritual Intimacy

Wives' Top Five Love Needs
1. Unconditional Love and Acceptance
2. Emotional Intimacy and Communication
3. Spiritual Intimacy
4. Encouragement and Affirmation
5. Companionship

7. On the lines below, write

    (a) your definition of each love need,
    (b) how it might show itself in a marriage, and
    (c) why it is important in a marriage.

Share your comments as a group.
Unconditional love and acceptance

(a) _____

(b) _____

(c) _____

Intimacy (Sexual [men] / Emotional [women])—(men answer for men; women answer for women)

(a) _____

(b) _____

(c) _____

Spiritual Intimacy

(a) _____

(b) _____

(c) _____

Encouragement / Affirmation

(a) _____

(b) _____

(c) _____

Companionship

(a) _____

(b) _____

(c) _____

8. What are some possible results that could occur if couples never meet each other's love needs?

_____

_____

SHARING AS A COUPLE

For this section, you and your spouse need to work together to answer the questions listed below.

We realize that you and your spouse may not fall in the same pattern as the majority of our survey. So now it's your turn. Rate these love needs from 1 to 5 for you, and then rate according to how you think your spouse will rate them.

My Top Five Love Needs	*My Spouse's Top Five Love Needs*
____ Companionship	____ Companionship
____ Encouragement/Affirmation	____ Encouragement/Affirmation
____ Intimacy (sexual/emotional)	____ Intimacy (sexual/emotional)
____ Spiritual intimacy	____ Spiritual intimacy
____ Unconditional love/acceptance	____ Unconditional love/acceptance

Turn to your spouse, and share with each other how you rated both lists of love needs. For now, just share the numbers you each placed beside each need—save the details for later discussion.

Is this how you thought your spouse would prioritize these needs? _____

If you weren't exactly right, don't panic. Most people aren't completely accurate in how they rate their spouses. After all, that's why you're here! Put the corrected list below. Then memorize it. You'll need it in the weeks to come (for that matter, you'll need it forever!).

My Spouse's Top Five Love Needs Are:

_____

_____

_____

_____

_____

Ask your spouse about a time when you met one of the above needs. Have him/her describe how it made him/her feel. Write that description below:

_____

_____

PREPARING FOR THE WEEK

As a group, study the following ground rules.

1. CONCENTRATE ON YOUR SPOUSE'S NEEDS

    Take the responsibility to "give" to your spouse, and trust that God will meet your own needs however he chooses. By being "other focused" and concerned about meeting your spouse's needs first, you may be surprised how God will bless you by involving your husband or wife in meeting each of your own needs.

2. AVOID CRITICISM

    When it comes time for your spouse to focus on your needs, be careful not to be critical of how he or she hasn't met your past needs. Never criticize your spouse to the group.

3. KEEP YOUR GROUP SHARING TIME SAFE

    Some, if not all, in your group will want to share the progress that each is making from week to week. Keep your sharing time confidential within your group, and avoid comparing each other's marriage relationships. Make your group a safe place to share your strengths and struggles.

4. Focus on "Being" as Well as "Doing"

Meeting our spouse's needs involves "doing" something. But our "doing" is empowered by our "being" something. As our attitudes are transformed, our behavior changes. So throughout this course you will be asked to focus on certain Christ-like attitudes that will direct your actions.

5. Complete Your Weekly Exercises and Assignments

Each week you will be asked to spend a couple of hours between these group sessions in discovering how to better meet your spouse's needs. This includes personal reflection time, couple interaction time, journaling time, plus time to read the assigned chapters.

During this week, you will study the love need of unconditional love, rated number 1 by both husbands and wives. Remember to do the three days of homework immediately following this lesson. This will include reading chapters 1 and 2 of The Five Love Needs of Men and Women.

End the meeting in prayer.

Week One—Day One

MY PERSONAL REFLECTION:
UNDERSTANDING
UNCONDITIONAL LOVE

During the week, read chapters 1 and 2 in *The Five Love Needs of Men and Women*. In chapter 1, Gary talks to wives about how their husbands feel the need for unconditional love; in chapter 2, Barb talks to husbands about how their wives feel the need for unconditional love. It will be useful for both of you to read both chapters.

To help your spouse understand what unconditional love means to you and when you need it most, answer the three questions listed below. Your spouse will be answering these same three questions from his or her perspective, and you will be sharing your answers with each other later this week.

1. What does unconditional love **sound** like to you? Check (✔) any phrase that applies, and then write out your own answer below in detail.

    ❏ "You did what!?"
    ❏ "You don't need to apologize, I really understand."
    ❏ "I don't even want to hear your excuses."
    ❏ "That's okay, honey."
    ❏ "I have no idea of what you were thinking."
    ❏ "It doesn't matter sweetheart, I love you."

    Complete the following:
    I need my spouse's unconditional love when I

    _____ _____

    _____ _____

    _____

Words that will express unconditional love to me are

_____

_____

_____

2. What does unconditional love **look** like to you? Check (✔) any phrase that
    applies, and then write out your own answer below in detail.

    ❑   A warm embrace
    ❑   Deafening silence
    ❑   A blank look
    ❑   A cold shoulder
    ❑   A reassuring smile
    ❑   A gentle kiss

    Actions that show that unconditional love to me are

    _____

    _____

    _____

3. When your spouse shows you a love without condition, it makes you **feel** a cer-
    tain way. Describe those feelings.

    _____

    _____

    _____

LEARNING TO SERVE THROUGH UNCONDITIONAL LOVE

Because we are human, we can never love unconditionally in the absolute and perfect
sense in which God loves us. But he is the love model we strive to replicate in our
marriages. Contemplate the depth of God's love and breadth of his grace for you by
completing these sentences.

4. God, I believe you would love me even if I

    _____

    _____

    _____

5. Sometimes, dear God, I don't feel I deserve your love because

_____

_____

_____

Would you be willing to share the above completed sentences with your spouse and explain how much it would mean to you if he or she could love you that way?

❑ Yes ❑ No ❑ Maybe ❑ I'm afraid how my spouse might answer

End this time of reflection by making the following prayer your own.

> Dear Father God, thank you for loving me without condition. It is by your grace that you have forgiven me. You humbled yourself by giving your Son as a sacrifice for me when I was a sinner. I fail, and you still keep on loving me. I sin, and you offer me continual forgiveness. May the grace you show me be the grace I extend to my spouse. Let your forgiveness be my forgiveness. Let your patience be my patience. Let your unselfish giving be my unselfish giving. Let your unselfish service be mirrored in me. And let your unfailing, unconditional love be shown through me. Amen.

Week One—Day Two

COUPLE INTERACTION:
SERVING MY SPOUSE WITH UNCONDITIONAL LOVE

You will need to set aside about thirty minutes to complete this exercise with your spouse. Be sure you have selected a place where you will not be interrupted (turn off the phones and pagers, and find a location that will allow you to comfortably share with each other).

This time is intended to help you

- understand how you can be part of God's plan of meeting your spouse's need for unconditional love;
- discover a way to practice meeting this need for your spouse;
- plan a time later this week to focus on meeting this need for your spouse.

How Does My Spouse Experience Unconditional Love?
Take turns sharing with each other how you completed your Personal Reflection questions. Say: "I truly want to know what unconditional love sounds, looks, and feels like to you in various situations." In the space provided below, take notes as you listen to what your spouse says:

To my spouse, unconditional love **sounds** like:

_____

_____

_____

_____

To my spouse, unconditional love **looks** like:

_____

_____

_____

_____

To my spouse, unconditional love **feels** like:

_____

_____

_____

_____

What fresh insight did you gain about meeting your spouse's need for a love without condition? Share that insight with your spouse, and express that you want your love saturated with grace so you can consistently love him or her no matter what.

_____

_____

_____

Talking It Over

Loving without condition is accepting your spouse for who he or she is, no matter what. Confessing to each other that you need the other's loving grace is a vital step in meeting each other's need for unconditional love.

Go back to the exercise "Learning to Serve through Unconditional Love" in the previous day's lesson and share how you completed questions 4 and 5. Now fill in your personal answers to the following questions, and then share them with your spouse.

_____(your spouse's name) I need to know you really love and accept me especially when I

_____

_____

_____

Sometimes _____(your spouse's name), I don't feel I deserve your love because

_____

_____

_____

_____

Pray this prayer together:

> Dear loving Father, as a couple we want to meet each other's need for
> unconditional love, but we need your help. You alone are the ultimate sup-
> plier of unconditional love. Let us sense your love for us right now so we
> can better love each other. Grant our love relationship your spirit of grace
> so we can meet each other's need for unconditional love. In Jesus' name,
> amen.

Week One—Day Three

MY ASSIGNMENT:
PRACTICING
UNCONDITIONAL LOVE

You have two assignments this week:

1. Read chapters 1 and 2 of *The Five Love Needs of Men and Women*.

    Have you completed that assignment yet?

    ❑ Yes   ❑ No   ❑ I've started, but I have more to read.

2. Practice meeting your spouse's need for unconditional love.

Your assignment (should you choose to accept it) is to understand how your spouse needs to experience your unconditional love and to practice doing that with patient, forgiving, unselfish love and sacrificial service. Record what you did or said and how your spouse responded.

Be creative and pro-active. You might want to surprise your mate with a date night. (If you need ideas, check out our book *40 Unforgettable Dates with Your Mate*, which is stocked with ideas for dates that will help you meet your spouse's love needs.) Or you may want to write a thoughtful poem or letter. Fulfilling this assignment needs to be something that expresses to your spouse that you love him/her without any strings attached. Journal below how it went and if you're comfortable. be prepared to report what happened to your small group later this week.

My Journal

Here is what I did and how it went when I practiced loving my spouse without condition this week.

_____

_____

_____

_____

_____

_____

_____

_____

Here is what I have learned about how I need to meet my spouse's need for unconditional love.

_____

_____

_____

_____

_____

_____

_____

_____

Group Session Two

LOVE THAT IS "FOR BETTER OR FOR WORSE" UNCONDITIONAL LOVE

SETTING THE MOOD

During the week, you and your spouse should have read chapters 1 and 2 of *The Five Love Needs of Men and Women*. Ideally you also made time to work through the home-work assignments so that you could discuss how unconditional love sounds, looks, and feels for each of you.

As the session begins, couples should work together to answer the following questions.

1. Describe a radio or television commercial that gives a great offer followed by a fast-talking announcer who spells out all of the "exceptions" to the deal. What types of exceptions are listed in the fine print for advertisements?

    _____

    _____

    _____

2. Great offers usually come with conditions. However, our love for our spouses should not, as you discovered this past week in your reading and in your home-work assignments. Describe some conditions (or fine print) that sometimes occur in marriages. How does conditional love weaken the marriage bond?

    _____

    _____

    _____

Unconditional guarantees are pretty hard to come by. There are always conditions— you must have the sales receipt, you must have proof of identity, you must have good credit, you must purchase within the next twenty-four hours, etc.

When you entered into your marriage, like it or not, you signed what God considers an unconditional guarantee. Even if you wrote your own vows, you probably said something like,

> for better or for worse,
> for richer or for poorer,
> in sickness and in health . . .

Those were more than just words; they were vows—promises, guarantees. You were saying, in essence,

> If things get better for us, I love you.
> If things get worse, I will love you.
> If we get rich beyond our wildest dreams, I will love you.
> If we grow poorer and don't own much, I will love you.
> If you get sick, I will love you.
> If you remain healthy, I will love you.
> In fact, no matter what happens, I will always love you.

DISCOVERING THE NEED FOR UNCONDITIONAL LOVE

We all have the need to love and be loved. In fact, our survey indicated that couples want a certain kind of love above all other kinds of love—unconditional love. This week, you looked in depth at the number one love need we discovered for both men and women: unconditional love.

This is not to assume that both you and your spouse placed this as your number one love need. As you work through this study with the five top love needs from our survey, you will be given the tools to discover how to meet your spouse's particular love needs as you targeted at the end of the last group session.

When you got married, you made a commitment to love unconditionally when you vowed to mutually love each other "for better or for worse, for richer or for poorer, in sickness and in health." That kind of love says, *"I'm going to love you for who you are. I'll look beyond your faults and failures and accept you for the person you are, warts and all."* We all need an unconditional love relationship, but we need it most when we deserve it least.

Unconditional love means loving and accepting a person— no matter what.

Gary says to wives:

Your response, initiative, and connection to your husband are crucial to the health of your marriage and family. Your expression of your unconditional love and acceptance is the very force that will drive you together in the midst of the testing times. . . . At times this means putting aside your own needs in order to meet his. . . . Your husband desperately needs to know that you will accept him no matter what. Even when he fails or makes poor decisions. Even when he feels crummy about himself or disappoints you. Your love is a make or break reality . . . Your unconditional love and acceptance will build him up and free him to go on. (pages 23-24)

Barb says to husbands:

When you love your wife unconditionally, you reflect God's love to her. . . . Your wife needs this kind of love most during times of pain. She needs you to surround her with your presence, your tenderness, and your desire to help her heal. . . . Fiery trials offer you an opportunity to put your own feet in the coals along with her and show your wife that you love her no matter what. Grab these opportunities to show your complete trust and devotion to her. God's Spirit is in you. Rely on him to teach you what to say, how to say it tenderly, and what to do. Lean on his understanding to become "God with skin on" to your wife. Unconditional love has the power to transform your wife. (page 40)

THE HEART ATTITUDE OF UNCONDITIONAL LOVE

One word that can aptly encompass the attitude of unconditional love is a heart full of **grace**.

> Do not let any part of your body become a tool of wickedness, to be used for sinning. Instead, give yourselves completely to God since you have been given new life. And use your whole body as a tool to do what is right for the glory of God. Sin is no longer your master, for you are no longer subject to the law, which enslaves you to sin. Instead, you are free by God's grace. (Romans 6:13-14)

3. What do these verses mean to you about living by God's grace?

_____

_____

_____

To meet your spouse's need for unconditional love requires that you exercise grace. Grace means you love him or her even when love at the moment doesn't seem warranted. Grace is the empowering force that makes love an unconditional quality in your marriage. Grace is the fertile ground in which love grows deep and secure. Grace is patient, forgiving, and unselfish.

We can develop more grace in our marriage relationship by going to the origin of grace—our relationship with God. The more we receive God's grace, the more grace we can impart to the one person we love most. Take a moment and reflect on the many ways God has shown you his grace.

4.   God has shown me his grace by

_____

_____

_____

Unconditional love is expressed in certain actions that look and sound a certain way. But such a love comes from an attitude of the heart.

5.   Read the following passage carefully, and list the heart attitudes in the spaces below (you should come up with nine). For example: the first one is *patient*. On the lines after each heart attitude, explain why you think this is important in expressing unconditional love.

> Love is patient and kind. Love is not jealous or boastful or proud or rude. Love does not demand its own way. Love is not irritable, and it keeps no record of when it has been wronged. (1 Corinthians 13:4-5)

_____ Patient _____

_____

_____

_____

_____

_____

_____

_____

_____

_____

Unconditional love is based on **a patient attitude** that endures another's weakness, **a forgiving heart** that doesn't hold grudges, **an unselfish spirit** that is willing to give of themselves, and so on. Unconditional love shows itself through **sacrificial serving**, putting your spouse ahead of yourself. These four attitudes empower us to love and keep on loving in the midst of another's faults and failings.

6. God shows us grace by loving us unconditionally, loving us even when we don't deserve it. How has God been:

patient with us?

_____

forgiving of us?

_____

unselfish toward us?

_____

sacrificially serving toward us?

_____

7. Spend a few minutes considering how you might be able to improve in exhibiting these qualities in your marriage. Rate yourself from 1 to 5 (1 is "I don't do this at all," and 5 is "I am consistently this way"). Then write how you might be able to raise your personal score.

Patient attitude

1   2   3   4   5

I could improve in the area of patience by

_____

_____

Forgiving heart

1   2   3   4   5

I could improve in the area of forgiveness by

_____

_____

_____

Unselfish spirit

| 1 | 2 | 3 | 4 | 5 |

I could improve in the area of unselfishness by

_____

_____

_____

Sacrificial serving

| 1 | 2 | 3 | 4 | 5 |

I could improve in the area of service by

_____

_____

_____

SHARING AS A COUPLE

For this section, you and your spouse need to work together in a semiprivate spot in the room to answer the following questions:

8. Share with each other the answers you gave to question 7.

9. What makes it difficult to love unconditionally?

_____

_____

_____

_____

10. In what ways can people resolve to erase the "fine print" in their marriages and give an unconditional guarantee of love to their spouses?

_____

_____

_____

_____

PREPARING FOR THE WEEK

During the coming week, you will study the love need of intimacy—especially as it relates to men. (The following week, we will focus on how women experience intimacy.) Remember to do the three days of homework immediately following this lesson. This will include reading chapter 3 of The Five Love Needs of Men and Women.

We realize that the topic of intimacy is—well—so intimate! *This may be a difficult topic to discuss and you may find it very unnatural to talk about some of these issues. We encourage you to remember, first of all, that this is your* spouse *we're talking about. You're together in this course seeking to learn how to meet each other's love needs. You can't do that for each other if you don't communicate your needs. So attempt to bring down the barriers, and be honest with each other. You'll be glad you did!*

End the meeting in prayer.

Week Two—Day One

MY PERSONAL REFLECTION: UNDERSTANDING MEN'S VIEW OF INTIMACY

During the week, read chapter 3 in *The Five Love Needs of Men and Women,* where Gary talks to wives about how their husbands feel the need for intimacy. Because men and women view intimacy so differently, we will study the topic of intimacy for two weeks. This week we will consider how men view intimacy; next week we'll look at how women view intimacy.

To help both husbands and wives understand what intimacy means to husbands, each of you need to read the following quotations from the book and answer the questions focused on you in the following sections. You will talk about your answers later this week.

Gary says to wives:
Men created males with a strong sex drive . . . Men also have the uncanny ability to compartmentalize their lives. We live in "boxes." We have a work box, a church box, a friend box, a sports box, a sex box, and so on. The sex box is always on the periphery of our lives, ready to be opened at a moment's notice.
(page 57)

Husbands answer the following questions:

1. Describe the different "boxes" in your life.

   _____

   _____

   _____

   _____

2. Do you find it easy to compartmentalize your life in these boxes? Explain.

_____

_____

_____

3. Do you agree with Gary that the other "boxes" in your life do not affect your desire to have sex with your wife? Why or why not?

_____

_____

_____

Wives answer the following questions:

1. Describe the different "boxes" in your husband's life.

_____

_____

_____

2. Do you think he finds it easy to compartmentalize his life in these different boxes? Explain.

_____

_____

_____

_____

3. Does it help you to understand that your husband's desire for sex is not necessarily affected by other things happening in your lives? Explain.

_____

_____

_____

_____

Gary says to wives:
Perhaps the most important fact you need to know is that a man finds much of his own masculinity in his sexuality . . . Sex, passion, pleasing the woman he loves . . . that's what makes a man feel like a man.
(page 57)

Husbands answer the following questions:

4. Do you agree with Gary's statement above? Why or why not?

    _____

    _____

    _____

5. How important is your sexual relationship with your wife?

    _____

    _____

    _____

Wives answer the following questions:

4. Have you understood the importance of the sexual relationship for your hus-
    band, or is this new information? Explain.

    _____

    _____

    _____

5. Do you feel that you and your husband are working together to meet his need
    for physical intimacy? Why or why not?

    _____

    _____

    _____

LEARNING TO SERVE THROUGH INTIMACY

God created both husbands and wives with the need for intimacy in marriage. While
it is true that men tend to focus on sexual intimacy and women tend to focus on
emotional intimacy, we both want the same thing. We want to experience something
deep and significant with our spouse, with the emphasis on *experience*.

   To do this means that you need to discover who your spouse really is and then
really love what you find. The word *intimacy* comes from a Latin word that means
"innermost." This means that in the marriage relationship there is a vulnerable sharing of your inner thoughts, feelings, spirits, bodies, and true selves. Both the husband
and wife need to feel secure that they can share these things with each other with
complete confidence of their spouse's acceptance and support (their unconditional
love!).

6. Do I feel comfortable really sharing myself with my spouse physically? Why or why not?

_____

_____

_____

7. Does my spouse feel comfortable sharing himself/herself physically with me? If there are some problem areas, what can I do to help?

_____

_____

_____

End this time of reflection by making the following prayer your own.

> Dear Lord, thank you for the attitude of self-sacrifice that you showed to me when you gave yourself for me. I know that in order to truly love my spouse, I need to also have an attitude of self-sacrifice—seeking to place his [her] needs above my own. I long for intimacy with my spouse—the one-ness that you promised when you created marriage. I ask that during this week, we will learn more about each other and deepen our intimacy. Thank you for making him [her] the perfect match for me. Teach us more about each other so that we can meet each other's needs for intimacy. Amen.

Week Two—Day Two

COUPLE INTERACTION:
SERVING MY SPOUSE WITH INTIMACY

You will need to set aside about thirty minutes to complete this exercise with your spouse. Be sure you have selected a place where you will not be interrupted (turn off the phones and pagers, and find a location that will allow you to comfortably share with each other).

This time is intended to help you:

- understand how your husband needs intimacy, and how you can work together to meet his need;
- discover a way to practice meeting this need for your spouse;
- plan a time later this week to focus on meeting this need for your husband.

How Does Your Husband Experience Intimacy?
Take turns sharing with each other how you completed your Personal Reflection questions. Discuss how your answers for questions 1-3 were similar or different. Do the same with questions 4 and 5.

What fresh insight did you gain about a husband's need for intimacy?

_____

_____

_____

_____

_____

TALKING IT OVER

Intimacy can be achieved in marriage. These attitudes can be developed in your lives so that you can move into your spouse's life and fulfill his/her needs for intimacy. You can know that this is possible because God will give you the ability to do so. No matter what you may be going through right now—what external or internal difficulties are facing your marriage—know that God wants to help you work together to deepen and strengthen your bond.

Share your answers to questions 6 and 7. Discuss what you can do for each other to meet the husband's need for physical intimacy. (Of course, wives desire physical intimacy as well but, as you have discovered, that desire can be dampened when their needs in other areas are not met. You'll look at that more in the next session.)

It is important to discuss each other's expectations and not draw your conclusions about how much you each desire sex from the latest *Cosmopolitan* cover at the grocery checkout. Husbands, talk about how often you would like to be able to have sex with your wife. Manage each other's expectations while taking into account the things that often get in the way (more on that in the next session as well). If you know each other's desires, that goes a long way to helping you set goals in order to meet each other's needs for physical intimacy.

Pray this prayer together:

> Dear loving Father, as a couple we want to meet each other's need for intimacy, but we need your help. Help us to draw closer together so that we can be "as one." You united us when we got married, Lord, if there are things in our pasts that are affecting our ability to have a God-honoring sexual relationship together, please bring your healing into our lives. Show us what we need to do to resolve those problems and become strong and unified before you. In Jesus' name, amen.

Week Two—Day Three

MY ASSIGNMENT:
PRACTICING INTIMACY

You have two assignments this week:

1. Read chapter 3 of *The Five Love Needs of Men and Women*.

    Have you completed that assignment yet?

    ❑ Yes   ❑ No   ❑ I've started, but I have more to read.

2. Practice meeting your spouse's need for physical intimacy.

Sometimes it's hard to bring back the spark if you're going through a difficult time. But you really need to work on this with each other, *especially* when you're going through a difficult time. Our book *40 Unforgettable Dates with Your Mate* can give you some ideas to get you started. Some of you don't need any prodding, but right now, set aside a date time when you both will plan on spending intimate time together. And don't break the date!

Our date this week will take place on: _____

My Journal

Here is what I have learned about how I need to meet my spouse's need for physical intimacy.

_____

_____

_____

_____

_____

_____

_____

_____

_____

_____

Group Session Three

THE TWO SHALL BE ONE
MEN AND INTIMACY

SETTING THE MOOD

During the week, you and your spouse should have read chapter 3 of *The Five Love Needs of Men and Women*. Ideally you also made time to work through the homework assignments so that you could discuss how the male half of your marriage understands and needs intimacy.

As the session begins, couples should work together to answer the following questions:

1. On the lines below, list pairs that go together naturally. Think of as many as you can. For example, "peanut butter and jelly" or "shoes and socks." At the end of the list, write the names of you and your spouse.

    _____ and _____
    _____ and _____
    _____ and _____
    _____ and _____
    _____ and _____
    And us: _____ and _____

2. In what ways do you think you and your spouse might look differently at the topic of intimacy? What is intimacy according to

    the wife _____?
    the husband _____?

33

Strong feelings for our spouse are part of what makes marriage so special to us. We can still remember what we felt when we first realized that we were falling in love. At times, we were overwhelmed by the emotional connection between us.

Today, we want to discuss how we can strengthen this connection with our spouse and experience "emotional oneness." Emotional oneness is our description of what God prescribes in Genesis 2:24, where he says,

> This explains why a man leaves his father and mother and is joined to his wife, and the two are united into one.

We know that we can connect emotionally with our spouse. Indeed, this is what we were doing last week when we completed our assignments. To achieve emotional oneness means that we are aware, on a daily basis, of our spouse's needs and we are searching for ways to meet those needs. It means that we are constantly exploring ways to get to know our spouse more intimately. Emotional oneness is a process of discovery that assumes that we still have more to learn about our spouse and we are excited about the prospect of deepening our intimacy. But, to do this requires that we develop certain key attitudes.

DISCOVERING THE NEED FOR PHYSICAL INTIMACY

We found it interesting that men and women gave different names to their number two love need, but that both different names boil down to a need for intimacy. The dictionary defines *intimacy* as "a close association with or deep understanding of." Those two aspects of intimacy dovetail exactly with the two different ways men and women think about the number two love need.

Intimacy means experiencing a deep emotional oneness with my spouse.

To put it very briefly and bluntly:

Men spell *intimacy*	S-E-X.
Women spell *intimacy*	T-A-L-K

In other words, for men, intimacy is the "close association" from the dictionary definition and for women, it is the "deep understanding." So husbands and wives need to understand how to meet each other's needs for intimacy by learning to be intimate in ways that "speak" to each other.

Because men and women view intimacy in such different ways, we're going to spend two weeks on this topic. Today we will look at how men view intimacy; next week we'll consider more in depth how women view intimacy.

Gary says to wives:

Perhaps the most important fact you need to know is that a man finds much of his own masculinity in his sexuality. This is part of our maleness; we can't erase it . . . Sex, passion, pleasing the woman he loves . . . that's what makes a man feel like a man . . . A fulfilled and vibrant sexual relationship is part of God's plan for a great marriage. That's why when a man and a woman are committed to oneness in their marriage, their sexual relationship only gets better . . . So enjoy your husband! Affirm him. Reach out to him. Study him and his needs. Communicate your love and passion for him. And experience deep pleasure in the safety of your marriage relationship.
(pages 57–58, 73–74)

THE HEART ATTITUDE OF PHYSICAL INTIMACY
Read the following Bible verses and answer the questions.

> This explains why a man leaves his father and mother and is joined to his wife, and the two are united into one. (Genesis 2:24)

3. How does sexual intimacy make two people into "one"?

_____

_____

_____

> Let your wife be a fountain of blessing for you. Rejoice in the wife of your youth. (Proverbs 5:18)

4. How can wives be "fountains of blessing" to their husbands?

_____

_____

_____

5. How can men "rejoice" in their wives?

_____

_____

_____

The husband should not deprive his wife of sexual intimacy, which is her right as a married woman, nor should the wife deprive her husband. (1 Corinthians 7:3)

6. What does Paul recommend that the spouses *not* do?

_____

_____

_____

7. Why is it dangerous for couples to "deprive" each other? What happens when the need for physical intimacy goes unmet?

_____

_____

_____

It is important for spouses to understand that sex was created by God and intended for pleasure. Sometimes men or women will come into the marriage carrying past baggage that has a profound effect on their ability to build sexual intimacy with their spouse. If that is true in your relationship, you need to seek God and then perhaps seek help from a Christian counselor who can help you work through these issues together.

Divide into separate groups—men in one, women in another. Discuss the following in your groups.

Men:
Look at the Proverbs 5:18 verse above. How can you show your wife that you "rejoice" in her—not just in your sexual relationship, but in all areas of your life together?

_____

_____

_____

Women:
Look at the Proverbs 5:18 verse above. How can you be a "fountain of blessing" to your husband—not just in your sexual relationship, but in all areas of your life together?

_____

_____

_____

SHARING AS A COUPLE

For this section, you and your spouse need to work together in a semiprivate spot in the room to answer the following questions:

8. Discuss the ramifications of *not* attempting to connect with physical intimacy on a regular basis. Describe these below.

    _____

    _____

    _____

9. Discuss the benefits of seeking to each other's love need for physical intimacy.

    _____

    _____

    _____

PREPARING FOR THE WEEK

During the coming week, you will study the women's view of the love need of intimacy. Remember to do the three days of homework immediately following this lesson. This will include reading chapter 4 of The Five Love Needs of Men and Women.

You learned this past week that men need to have physical intimacy with their wives. It's simply part of their wiring, part of the way God made them. When a wife meets her husband's need for physical intimacy, she is meeting his love need and making him feel like he's "king of the world"!

Now men, it's the husband's turn to focus on his wife this week. We're going to learn what makes women tick when it comes to intimacy.

End the meeting in prayer.

Week Three—Day One

MY PERSONAL REFLECTION: UNDERSTANDING WOMEN'S VIEW OF INTIMACY

During the week, read chapter 4 in *The Five Love Needs of Men and Women,* where Barb talks to husbands about how their wives feel the need for intimacy. Last week we discussed how men view intimacy; this week we'll consider how women view intimacy.

To help both husbands and wives understand what intimacy means to wives, each of you need to read the following quotations from the book and answer the questions focused on you in the following sections. You will talk about your answers later this week.

Barb says to husbands:

Men are by nature compartmentalized creatures. Figuratively speaking, you view your work, your family, your hobbies, and your recreation as separate boxes . . . Men go through their entire day with each box standing alone, unconnected. Women are totally different! We go through the same activities, but each box has an invisible, emotional thread connecting them all together . . . When one box is affected, there is a chain reaction that ultimately affects our spirits.
(page 78)

Wives answer the following questions:
1.   Describe the different "boxes" in your life.

   _____

   _____

   _____

2. Do you find it difficult to separate how your emotions react to these different boxes? Explain.

_____

_____

_____

3. Does it help you to understand that your emotions in one area of life may have everything to do with what's happening in another area? Explain.

_____

_____

_____

Husbands answer the following questions:

1. Describe the different "boxes" in your wife's life.

_____

_____

_____

2. Do you think she finds it difficult to separate how her emotions react to these different boxes? Explain.

_____

_____

_____

3. Does it help you to understand that your wife's emotions in one area of life may have everything to do with what's happening in another area? Explain.

_____

_____

_____

_____

Barb says to husbands:

Emotional intimacy is so rich, so fulfilling for a woman. It doesn't replace the need for sex, but for her, the emotional need is as intense as the physical need. And when that need is fulfilled by her husband and sustained through thoughtful T-A-L-K time, it is much easier for her to move more quickly into a sexual mode.

(page 79)

Wives answer the following questions:

4. Do you agree with Barbara's statement above? Why or why not?

    _____

    _____

    _____

5. How important is your emotional relationship with your husband? How much do you need him to talk to you?

    _____

    _____

    _____

Husbands answer the following questions:

4. Have you understood the importance of the emotional relationship for your wife, or is this new information? Explain.

    _____

    _____

    _____

5. Do you feel that you are treating your wife like your "best customer"—in other words, giving her the attention she deserves? Why or why not?

    _____

    _____

    _____

LEARNING TO SERVE THROUGH INTIMACY

As you learned in the last lesson, God created both husbands and wives with the need for intimacy in marriage. Men tend to focus on sexual intimacy, and women tend to focus on emotional intimacy. Both needs are equally important and equally legitimate.

Just as marriage partners vulnerably share their bodies in the sexual realm, they also vulnerably share the rest of their lives. Men need to understand that women *want* to hear about their day. Wives *want* to know what happened at work, over lunch, on the court, wherever. They thrive on the details. They want to get into their husbands' world. So let's spend some time getting to know each other a little bit better.

6. How well does your spouse know you? On the lines below, write three things that you think he/she doesn't know. This can be from any time frame in your life

and on any topic. You will share these with your spouse in your Couple Interaction time.

Three Things My Spouse May Not Know about Me

(a) _____

(b) _____

(c) _____

7. How well do you know your spouse? Think of three questions you'd like to ask your spouse. Again, this can be about any time frame in his/her life and on any topic. You will ask these questions in your Couple Interaction time.

Three Things I'd Like to Know about My Spouse

(a) _____

(b) _____

(c) _____

End this time of reflection by making the following prayer your own.

> Dear Lord, thank you for the attitude of self-sacrifice that you showed to me when you gave yourself for me. I know that in order to truly love my spouse, I need to also have an attitude of self-sacrifice—seeking to place his [her] needs above my own. I long for intimacy with my spouse—the one-ness that you promised when you created marriage. I ask that during this week, we will learn more about each other and deepen our intimacy. Thank you for making him [her] the perfect match for me. Teach us more about each other so that we can meet each other's needs for intimacy. Amen.

Week Three—Day Two

COUPLE INTERACTION:
SERVING MY SPOUSE
WITH INTIMACY

You will need to set aside about thirty minutes to complete this exercise with your spouse. Be sure you have selected a place where you will not be interrupted (turn off the phones and pagers, and find a location that will allow you to comfortably share with each other).

This time is intended to help you

- understand how your wife needs intimacy and how you can work together to meet her need;
- discover a way to practice meeting this need for your spouse;
- plan a time later this week to focus on meeting this need for your wife.

How Does Your Wife Experience Intimacy?
Take turns sharing with each other how you completed your Personal Reflection questions. Discuss how your answers for questions 1-3 were similar or different. Do the same with questions 4 and 5.

What fresh insight did you gain about a wife's need for intimacy?

_____

_____

_____

_____

_____

Talking It Over

Because the need for intimacy differs between husbands and wives, you both need to consider and take seriously each other's needs. The husband's desire for S-E-X doesn't mean he has a one-track mind. The wife's need for T-A-L-K doesn't make the husband into nothing more than one of her girlfriends. Instead, when you both understand each other's distinct needs, how those need contribute to intimacy in your marriage, and how meeting those needs often insures that your own needs will be met in return—then you'll be ready to work at this with all that much more enthusiasm!

Share your answers to questions 6 and 7. Have fun learning more about each other!

Pray this prayer together:

> Dear loving Father, as a couple we want to meet each other's need for intimacy, but we need your help. Help us to draw closer together so that we can be "as one." You united us when we got married, Lord, now help us to build on that unity by remaining intimate friends. In Jesus' name, amen.

Week Three—Day Three

MY ASSIGNMENT:
PRACTICING INTIMACY

You have two assignments this week:

1. Read chapter 4 of *The Five Love Needs of Men and Women*.

    Have you completed that assignment yet?

    ☐ Yes   ☐ No   ☐ I've started, but I have more to read.

2. Practice meeting your spouse's need for intimacy.

Men, your wives need emotional intimacy every day. Discuss with your wife how you can meet her need. Does she need a few minutes of talk as soon as you and she get home? Is it better to make a commitment to sit down and talk for thirty minutes after you put the children to bed? How about over breakfast or during the day on the phone?

In order to connect with each other, we will work to have T-A-L-K time each day at _____.

My Journal

Here is what I have learned about how I need to meet my spouse's need for emotional intimacy.

_____

_____

Group Session Four

JUST TALK TO ME
WOMEN AND INTIMACY

SETTING THE MOOD

During the week, you and your spouse should have read chapter 4 of *The Five Love Needs of Men and Women*. Ideally you also made time to work through the homework assignments so that you could discuss how the female half of your marriage understands and needs intimacy.

As the session begins, couples should work together to answer the following questions:

1. Describe your routines at the end of the day—when work is over, when kids are in bed, etc.

_____

_____

_____

_____

_____

2. How many minutes do you spend talking together each day? Is that enough, or would you like more?

_____

_____

_____

_____

DISCOVERING THE NEED FOR EMOTIONAL INTIMACY

As we discussed last week, men and women gave different names to their number two love need, but both names boil down to a need for intimacy. Here is the definition again:

Intimacy means experiencing a deep emotional oneness with my spouse.

We learned last week that men spell *intimacy* S-E-X.
We will discuss today how women spell *intimacy* T-A-L-K.

Barb says to husbands:

Your sex drive is connected to your eyes; you become aroused visually. Your wife's sex drive is connected to her heart; she is aroused only after she feels emotional closeness and harmony. You compartmentalize sex from everything else in your life. Your wife sees everything connected to everything else. You feel less masculine if your wife resists your sexual advances. Your wife feels like a machine if she doesn't experience sexual intimacy flowing from emotional intimacy . . . Your wife has an intense drive to be emotionally transparent with you. She needs to know everything about you. Not so that she can possess or control you, but so that she can experience true oneness with you. That's what intimacy is on the deepest level: when you let her get into your soul and you get into hers, when together you reveal who you are to each other, when you talk about everything and anything, when you share your opinions and perspectives.
(pages 77, 88)

THE HEART ATTITUDE OF INTIMACY

Read Philippians 2:1-8.

> Is there any encouragement from belonging to Christ? Any comfort from his love? Any fellowship together in the Spirit? Are your hearts tender and sympathetic? Then make me truly happy by agreeing wholeheartedly with each other, loving one another, and working together with one heart and purpose. Don't be selfish; don't live to make a good impression on others. Be humble, thinking of others as better than yourself. Don't think only about your own affairs, but be interested in others, too, and what they are doing. Your attitude should be the same that Christ Jesus had. Though he was God, he did not demand and cling to his rights as God. He made himself nothing; he took the humble position of a slave and appeared in human form. And in human form he obediently humbled himself even further by dying a criminal's death on a cross. (Philippians 2:1-8)

3. The apostle Paul wants the believers in Philippi to find encouragement, comfort, and fellowship with one another in the church. What does he recommend that they do?

    _____

    _____

    _____

4. How can we look to Jesus as our example in "not thinking only about our own affairs, but being interested in others, too"—namely, our spouses?

    _____

    _____

    _____

Identifying the barriers to emotional oneness in marriage is the first step toward achieving it. There are many reasons why this is difficult for married couples, but for the most part the reasons are very common among all couples. Let's think about these for a moment. Look at the passage above from the opposite perspective.

5. What does Paul recommend that the believers *not* do?

    _____

    _____

6. Translate the above into your marriage. What should you *not* do because it will affect the closeness in your marriage?

    _____

    _____

7. In the left-hand column below, list some obstacles to intimacy and oneness that you see occurring in marriages today. In the middle column, list an attitude or circumstance of life that contributes to that obstacle. In the last column, list what a person might do in order to overcome that obstacle. (One has been suggested.)

Obstacles to Intimacy	Attitude/Circumstance	A Way to Overcome It
Time	_Busyness of life_	_Scheduling time together_
_____	_____	_____
_____	_____	_____
_____	_____	_____

8. Divide into separate groups—men in one, women in another. Discuss in your groups what you might be able to do in order to connect with your spouse on a more intimate level on a more regular basis: Following are some suggestions. Write other ideas below.

Take thirty minutes at the end of every day to talk.

Set aside a date night every couple of weeks—and don't break the date.

Put aside some time that I spend on my hobby to spend with my spouse.

_____

_____

_____

SHARING AS A COUPLE

For this section, you and your spouse need to work together in a semiprivate spot in the room to answer the following questions:

9. Discuss the ramifications of *not* attempting to have emotional intimacy with each other on a regular basis. Describe these below.

_____

_____

_____

10. Discuss the benefits of seeking to meet your wife's love need for emotional intimacy.

_____

_____

_____

11. Choose one of the ideas from the list you made in the small groups (question 8), and tell your spouse that you are going to do that this week.

PREPARING FOR THE WEEK

During the coming week, you will study the love need of companionship. Remember to do the three days of homework immediately following this lesson. This will include reading chapters 5 and 10 of The Five Love Needs of Men and Women.

The idea of spouses as companions and friends is so simple that it seems almost not worth mentioning. Yet it ranks in the top five love needs for both men and women. Think about it—when you don't feel like friends, you're certainly not going to feel like lovers. Friendship is a key foundation for your relationship. If you've lost that key somewhere, it's time this week to go search for it. When you find it again, you'll discover that it will unlock doorways to great depth in your marriage.

This week is your opportunity to cultivate a more significant friendship with your spouse. In fact, the goal of this week's lesson is that you will make a commitment to become your spouse's best friend. If you already are your spouse's best friend, then your goal is to clearly identify with your spouse the reasons why you are best friends. In the process you will affirm and encourage this friendship.

End the meeting in prayer.

Week Four—Day One

MY PERSONAL REFLECTION:
UNDERSTANDING COMPANIONSHIP

During this week, read chapters 5 and 10 in *The Five Love Needs of Men and Women*. In chapter 5, Gary talks to wives about their husbands feel the need for companionship; in chapter 10, Barb talks to husbands about how their wives feel the need for companionship. It will be useful for both of you to read both chapters.

To help your spouse understand what companionship means to you and when you need it most, answer the following three questions. Your spouse will be answering these same three questions from his or her perspective and you will be sharing your answers with each other later this week.

1. What does companionship **sound** like to you? (Select the statements that apply, or write your own.)

    ❏ "What about your job gives you the most satisfaction?"
    ❏ "It is so good to be home with you. This is my favorite part of the day."
    ❏ "What do you think our children's greatest strengths and weaknesses are?"
    ❏ "My day just isn't the same without you right smack in the middle of it."
    ❏ "I missed you today."
    ❏ "I really value your wisdom and insight."
    ❏ "What would you like to do today?"
    ❏ _____
    ❏ _____
    ❏ _____

2. What does companionship **look** like to you? (Select the statements that apply or write your own.)

❏ Joining me in my favorite hobby or interest.
❏ Watching my favorite sport with me.
❏ Running errands with me.
❏ Going away for the weekend together.
❏ Taking a walk with me.
❏ Exercising with me.
❏ _____
❏ _____
❏ _____

3. When your spouse shows you companionship, it makes you **feel** a certain way. Describe those feelings.

_____

_____

_____

LEARNING TO SERVE THROUGH COMPANIONSHIP
4. In what activities would you like to have your spouse's companionship?

_____

_____

_____

5. What are your spouse's interests and/or hobbies? In what ways can you join him/her?

_____

_____

_____

6. Is your spouse your best friend? Why or why not?

_____

_____

_____

7. What can you do to strengthen your companionship/friendship with your spouse?

_____

_____

_____

End this time of reflection by making the following prayer your own.

> Dear Jesus, thank you for being my very best friend. Thank you for all that you did for us in order to allow us to be your friends. I pray for my marriage today, Lord, asking that you would rebuild the companionship we once knew so well and strengthen the bonds of our friendship.
>
> Teach us what it means to be each other's friends. Remind us how we should treat each other. Show us ways that we can become companions. Give us insight as we continue to learn more about each other. Amen.

Week Four—Day Two

COUPLE INTERACTION:
SERVING MY SPOUSE WITH COMPANIONSHIP

You will need to set aside about thirty minutes to complete this exercise with your spouse. Be sure you have selected a place where you will not be interrupted (turn off the phones and pagers, and find a location that will allow you to comfortably share with each other).

This time is intended to help you:

- understand how you can be part of God's plan of meeting your spouse's need for companionship;
- discover a way to practice meeting this need for your spouse;
- plan a time later this week to focus on meeting this need for your spouse.

HOW DOES MY SPOUSE EXPERIENCE COMPANIONSHIP?
Take turns sharing with each other how you completed your Personal Reflection questions.

To my spouse, companionship **sounds** like:

_____

_____

_____

_____

To my spouse, companionship **looks** like:

_____

_____

_____

_____

To my spouse, companionship **feels** like:

_____

_____

_____

_____

What fresh insight did you gain about meeting your spouse's need for companionship? Share that insight with your spouse, and express that you want to be his/her best friend.

_____

_____

_____

_____

TALKING IT OVER

Go back to the exercise "Learning to Serve through Companionship" in the previous day's assignment. Share the activities that you would like to have your spouse take part in with you. Then have your spouse share with you.

My spouse would like me to join him/her in _____

_____

Share your answers to questions 6 and 7. Discuss what you can do to strengthen your companionship/friendship with each other.

One thing I will do this week to help meet my spouse's need for companionship is _____

Pray this prayer together:

Dear Jesus, we want to honor you in our marriage. We want to recapture the friendship that we had when we first met. Rekindle our love, Lord. Deepen it and strengthen it. Show us what it means to truly be each other's favorite companion. In Jesus' name, Amen.

Week Four—Day Three

MY ASSIGNMENT:
PRACTICING COMPANIONSHIP

You have two assignments this week:

1. Read chapters 5 and 10 of *The Five Love Needs of Men and Women*.

   Have you completed that assignment yet?

   ❑ Yes   ❑ No   ❑ I've started, but I have more to read.

2. Practice meeting your spouse's need for companionship.

Your assignment this week is to find an opportunity to do one of the things that you and your spouse discussed in the Couple Interaction time. Spend some time this week being each other's best friends.

My Journal

Here is what I did and how it went when I practiced being a companion to my spouse this week.

_____

_____

_____

_____

_____

_____

_____

_____

_____

_____

Here is what I learned about how I need to meet my spouse's need for companion-ship.

_____

_____

_____

_____

_____

_____

_____

_____

_____

_____

Group Session Five

DISCOVERING YOUR BEST FRIEND
COMPANIONSHIP

SETTING THE MOOD

During the week, you and your spouse should have read chapters 5 and 10 of *The Five Love Needs of Men and Women*. Ideally you also made time to work through the homework assignments so that you could discuss how companionship sounds, looks, and feels for each of you.

As the session begins, couples should work together to answer the following questions.

1. Describe for each other what you like to do when you get together with your same-sex friends.

   Husband:

   _____

   Wife:

   _____

2. What were some of the activities you enjoyed doing together back when (*way back when*) you were dating? List some of those common interests below.

   _____

   _____

   _____

3. What types of activities do you still do together—just for fun, just to spend time together?

    _____

    _____

    _____

Friendship comes in a variety of forms. You probably have several different levels of friends in your circle. Outside of your spouse, you probably have a couple of very close friends. Then you have a circle of pretty good friends. Then you have the "back fence" friends—the people who are your friends by proximity, but perhaps you don't socialize with them except over the back fence.

You probably have friends that span the years, such as high-school or college friends whom you only hear from at holiday times, but it feels as if no time has passed. When you get together at a reunion, you pick up where you left off ten, twenty, even thirty years ago.

You probably have friends who span the world and friends who have moved away (or from whom you've moved away), but you share common experiences that keep you close.

How do you stay in touch with those people? You probably e-mail, send cards of encouragement, place a phone call, go out to lunch.

So where does your spouse fit in? That friendship began many years ago and has spanned the time from then until now—along with various joys, sorrows, and crises along the way. You have weathered much together. Sometimes that very familiarity takes its toll on the friendship. You forget to do those special things that show you care. Do you send the e-mails, cards of encouragement, place phone calls at work (just for fun—not to remind each other about who's to pick up the kids), or go out to lunch?

Like any other friendship, your friendship with your spouse needs to be nour-ished. That's why the love need for companionship is so important in marriage.

DISCOVERING THE NEED FOR COMPANIONSHIP

In our survey, the need for companionship came in as the number three love need for men and the number five love need for women.

Companionship, true friendship, happens when the marriage is comfortable and you enjoy each other's company.

4. When you hear the word *friendship,* what comes to mind? When you get together with your same-sex friends, what do you do? As a group, have the men give their answers, and then have the women give their answers.

<u>Men</u>	<u>Women</u>

5. What differences, if any, do you see between how men view friendship and how women view friendship?

_____

_____

_____

Gary says to wives:
Sadly, I have seen a pattern over and over in the counseling room. A man and woman fall in love romantically, commit to each other in marriage, but lack the depth of friendship love in their relationship. . . . True friendship, which involves trust and vulnerability, honesty and encouragement, shared interests and activities, takes time to develop and mature. And friendship between marriage partners requires the same. I call it "the velveteen rabbit syndrome." By the time our hair is rubbed off and our eyes go bad, we're finally comfortable with each other. We're comfortable enough to say what we need to say and be what we need to be with honor and grace and without condemnation. . . . Step closer to your husband by stepping into his world and enjoying the passions of his life. While his choice of recreation or relaxation may not be your first choice of the way to spend an afternoon or a vacation, he is your first choice.
(pages 102, 104, 110)

Barb says to husbands:
Friendship with your wife is an enjoyable process and a threshold to discovering new aspects of her. It reinforces what is already there and strengthens the marriage bond. A good friendship with your spouse lays the foundation to support other areas of your marriage relationship. Other areas of marriage may fluctuate over the years, but the friendship factor is lasting. . . . Couples who display a strong willingness to work hard at their marriage maintain the ability to laugh together, play together, stay the course together, and work through the inevitable differences. . . . Our need for your friendship and companionship is deeply intertwined with fulfilling the need for security and trust. . . . I encourage you to give your wife

a sense of deep security in your friendship. Build your friendship with such stability that when you face the tough times, you will find comfort and peace in your relationship with each other.
(pages 195–197, 207)

THE HEART ATTITUDE OF COMPANIONSHIP

The book of Proverbs is a rich resource on what friendship means. Apparently King Solomon had his share of interesting friends, and he learned some important lessons along the way.

6. Below each verse, write how this advice applies to your friendship with your spouse.

> Evil words destroy one's friends; wise discernment rescues the godly (11:9).

_____

_____

_____

> A troublemaker plants seeds of strife; gossip separates the best of friends (16:28).

_____

_____

_____

> Disregarding another person's faults preserves love; telling about them separates close friends (17:9).

_____

_____

_____

> A friend is always loyal, and a brother is born to help in time of need (17:17).

_____

_____

_____

_____

Just as damaging as a mad man shooting a lethal weapon is someone who lies to a friend and then says, "I was only joking" (26:18-19).

_____

_____

_____

Wounds from a friend are better than many kisses from an enemy (27:6).

_____

_____

_____

The heartfelt counsel of a friend is as sweet as perfume and incense (27:9).

_____

_____

_____

_____

As iron sharpens iron, a friend sharpens a friend (27:17).

_____

_____

_____

_____

Based on these verses, we could boil friendship down into three key words:

- **Honor**—who my spouse is, how God created him/her.
- **Loyalty**—to my spouse as an equal and valuable partner.
- **Compassion**—that looks past my spouse's faults and focuses on his/her strengths.

Consider as a group how couples can treat each other in these ways, then rate yourself in each area on a scale from 1 to 5 (1 being low, 5 being high).

7. How can married couples **honor** to each other?

_____

_____

_____

Rate your "honor factor." Do you appreciate your spouse's character and personal qualities? Do you make it a point to compliment your spouse on his/her good qualities—to him/her, as well as to others?

1   2   3   4   5

8. How can married couples exhibit **loyalty** to each other?

_____

_____

_____

Rate your "loyalty factor." Are you loyal (faithful) to your spouse emotionally, spiritually, and physically? Do you view your spouse as an equal and valuable partner in your life? Are you able to give and receive constructive criticism so that both of you become better people and your marriage becomes stronger?

1   2   3   4   5

9. How can married couples show **compassion** to each other?

_____

_____

_____

Rate your "compassion factor." Do you overlook faults and failures, or do you keep a mental list of every disappointment? Do you hurt when he/she hurts, feel joy when he/she feels joy? When there is a need, are you there to help?

1   2   3   4   5

While honor looks at the positive qualities and potential of another, compassion overlooks the faults or, at times, works through them together in order to become better people. The context of loyalty and "stick-to-it-iveness" in your marriage provides the safe place where all of this can happen. Make it a priority to work toward the attitudes of honor, loyalty, and compassion in your marriage. Who wouldn't want a friend like that?

SHARING AS A COUPLE

For this section, you and your spouse need to work together in a semiprivate spot in the room to answer the following questions.

10. Together share your answers to questions 7, 8, and 9. Discuss how you can begin to show honor, loyalty, and compassion toward each other. Take notes below.

_____

_____

_____

_____

PREPARING FOR THE WEEK

During the coming week, you will study the love need of encouragement and affirmation. Remember to do the three days of homework immediately following this lesson. This will include reading chapters 7 and 8 of The Five Love Needs of Men and Women.

Perhaps you were never a cheerleader (few of us were!). But now's your chance—and you don't even have to be able to do the jumps, build the pyramids, or learn the routines. You just need to find the right cheer to go with the right situation—words of cheer that will encourage your spouse, letting him/her know that you're there, you notice, you appreciate, and you love.

Sometimes, that's all you need to know.

End the meeting in prayer.

Week Five—Day One

MY PERSONAL REFLECTION: UNDERSTANDING ENCOURAGEMENT

During this week, read chapters 7 and 8 in *The Five Love Needs of Men and Women*. In chapter 7, Gary talks to wives about how husbands feel the need for encouragement and affirmation; in chapter 8, Barb talks to husbands about how wives feel the need for encouragement and affirmation. It will be useful for both of you to read both chapters.

To help your spouse understand what encouragement and affirmation mean to you and when you need it most, answer the following three questions. Your spouse will be answering these same three questions from his or her perspective, and you will be sharing your answers with each other later this week.

1. What does encouragement **sound** like to you? List the kinds of statements that encourage you.

   I am encouraged when my spouse says

   _____

   _____

   _____

2. What does encouragement **look** like to you? List actions that encourage you:
   I am encouraged when my spouse

   _____

   _____

   _____

3. When your spouse encourages you, it makes you **feel** a certain way. Describe those feelings.

_____

_____

_____

Learning to Serve through Encouragement

Consider a difficult situation that you and your spouse are currently facing. Perhaps it is a conflict with someone, a concern over a child, financial worries, job loss, etc. Briefly describe it below.

_____

_____

_____

4. In general, how are you reacting to that difficulty?

_____

_____

_____

5. How is your spouse reacting to the difficulty?

_____

_____

_____

6. How do you need encouragement from your spouse in order to deal with this difficulty?

_____

_____

_____

7. How do you think your spouse could use your encouragement during this difficult time?

_____

_____

_____

End this time of reflection by making the following prayer your own.

> Dear Lord, help me to be an encouragement to my spouse. There are so many things I appreciate about him [her]; remind me to say thank you. Show me what I can do to offer affirmation. In our current difficulty, Lord, help me to understand how my spouse is feeling. Help me to be an encouragement and to offer hope in our bleak situation. Help me to trust in you. Amen.

Week Five—Day Two

COUPLE INTERACTION:
SERVING MY SPOUSE WITH ENCOURAGEMENT

You will need to set aside about thirty minutes to complete this exercise with your spouse. Be sure you have selected a place where you will not be interrupted (that means turn off the phones and pagers, and find a location that will allow you to comfortably share with each other).

This time is intended to help you:

- understand how you can be part of God's plan of meeting your spouse's need for encouragement and affirmation;
- discover a way to practice meeting this need for your spouse;
- plan a time later this week to focus on meeting this need for your spouse.

HOW DOES MY SPOUSE EXPERIENCE ENCOURAGEMENT?
Take turns sharing with each other how you completed your Personal Reflection questions.

To my spouse, encouragement **sounds** like:

_____
_____
_____
_____
_____
_____

To my spouse, encouragement **looks** like:

_____

_____

_____

_____

To my spouse, encouragement **feels** like:

_____

_____

_____

_____

What fresh insight did you gain about meeting your spouse's need for encouragement? Share that insight with your spouse, and express that you want to encourage and affirm him/her every day.

_____

_____

_____

_____

Talking It Over

Go back to the exercise "Learning to Serve through Encouragement" in the previous day's assignment. Discuss the current difficult situation in your life, and then share your answers to questions 4 through 7.

Complete the following sentence:

One thing I will do this week to help meet my spouse's need for encouragement is _____

Pray this prayer together:

Dear loving Father, we truly want to meet each other's need for encouragement and affirmation. Sometimes it's hard—especially when we're in the middle of a tough situation. Give us the strength to look beyond the situation and value our relationship with each other. Teach us how to encourage each other. Amen.

Week Five—Day Three

MY ASSIGNMENT:
PRACTICING ENCOURAGEMENT

You have two assignments this week:

1. Read chapters 7 and 8 of *The Five Love Needs of Men and Women*.

   Have you completed that assignment yet?

   ❏ Yes   ❏ No   ❏ I've started, but I have more to read.

2. Practice meeting your spouse's need for encouragement.

When you think about it, right in the middle of the word *encouragement* is the word *courage*. Isn't that what encouragement does? It gives us the courage to go on—to run the race, to keep trying, to hang in there—especially when things are tough. Marriage isn't easy. You're bound to be blindsided by tough situations that will require courage from one or both of you.

My Journal

Here is what I did and how it went when I practiced encouraging my spouse this week.

_____

_____

_____

_____

_____

_____

_____

_____

_____

_____

Here is what I have learned about how I need to meet my spouse's need for encouragement.

_____

_____

_____

_____

_____

_____

_____

_____

_____

_____

Group Session Six

YOUR OWN PRIVATE CHEERING SECTION
ENCOURAGEMENT

SETTING THE MOOD

During the week, you and your spouse should have read chapters 7 and 8 of *The Five Love Needs of Men and Women*. Ideally you also made time to work through the homework assignments so that you could discuss how encouragement sounds, looks, and feels for each of you.

As the session begins, couples should work together to answer the following questions:

1. Make a list of the things you really appreciate about each other—the things you can "cheer on" in your spouse's character, strengths, gifts, etc. Then share your lists with each other.

    _____   _____
    _____   _____
    _____   _____
    _____   _____
    _____   _____
    _____   _____

2.   Now make a list of the things you would like to thank your spouse for
     being/doing. Share your lists with each other.

_____   _____

_____   _____

_____   _____

_____   _____

_____   _____

_____   _____

Remember those high school pep rallies? Remember doing the wave, holding up the
cards, clapping and yelling until you were hoarse? The team *needed* you—where
would they be if there were no spectators, no one to cheer them on? So you did your
fair share of yelling, "Let's go, Tigers, Let's go! (clap, clap)," over and over and over
again.

Perhaps you were out on the field or on the court. What did it mean to you to
have that great big cheering section? Maybe you were so intent on the game, you
barely heard them. But just knowing they were there was an encouragement in itself.

Each of you is out on the field at times, while the other is in the stands. Your husband has to be on the "field" of his job, his other commitments, his church activities,
his relationships with his kids. Your wife may also have the "field" of her job, as well as
your home, her activities, her involvements in the school or the church, her side
business, whatever. And the person on the field at any given moment needs to know
that the cheering section is going at it—wildly and with enthusiasm. "Let's go! You
can do it! You're the best! I'm proud of you!"

The cheering section is especially important when the tide is turning against one
of you for some reason. Perhaps it's a difficult boss, a rebellious child, or a misunder-
standing with another person. Each of you needs to be the private cheering section
for the other—encouraging and affirming as loudly as you can!

DISCOVERING THE NEED FOR ENCOURAGEMENT

Everyone needs encouragement. Think back across your lifetime. The favorite people
in your life—parents, teachers, mentors—were those who encouraged you, believed
in you, cheered you on, affirmed your accomplishments. That need never changes.

**Encouragement means that you are behind your spouse
all the way, believing in him/her, cheering him/her on.**

Both husbands and wives need encouragement from each other, and in our survey both men and women rated encouragement as their number four love need. Because men and women are different, encouragement needs to take different forms.

Gary says to wives:

Men still need to know they have a few fans left. . . . If you look up the word encouragement *in several dictionaries, you will find synonyms such as these: to cheer, comfort, hearten, inspire, buoy up, boost, invigorate, put one on top of the world, rejoice the heart, do the heart good. Do you realize what it would do for your marriage relationship if you did all those things for your husband? . . . Men are really struggling today. . . .When we men are in the midst of such trials, pushing our limits, we need to hear the voice of God leading and sustaining us, and we need to hear our wives encouraging and believing in us. Continually work to be a strong presence in your husband's world. Remind him of his worth in God's eyes, as well as to you and your children. Build him up. Cheer him on.*

(pages 145, 147, 155–56)

Barb says to husbands:

Women spend so much time supporting, helping, and nurturing the people in their lives, but they don't always get the support, help and nurture that they need in return. Because each woman is unique, you need to be a student of your own wife. . . . Understanding her personality and character will allow you to tailor your encouragement specifically for her. . . . Nothing will encourage your wife more than for you to recognize her sacrifices and affirm her love and devotion to your family. Think about it: She would do anything to strengthen and support you and your kids, right? She often does this so you can get ahead in your career. Encouragement from you will serve as a continual reminder to her that it's all worth it.

(pages 162, 170)

THE HEART ATTITUDE OF ENCOURAGEMENT

Read the following verses, and answer the questions.

> When I pray, you answer me; you encourage me by giving me the strength I need. (Psalm 138:3)

3. How did David describe God's encouragement? Why do you think he felt encouraged?

_____

_____

_____

> Don't use foul or abusive language. Let everything you say be good and
> helpful, so that your words will be an encouragement to those who hear
> them. (Ephesians 4:29)

4. How can we make sure that everything we say is "good and helpful"?

_____

_____

_____

> Think of ways to encourage one another to outbursts of love and good
> deeds. (Hebrews 10:24)

5. What kind of encouragement stimulates someone to "outbursts of love and good
   deeds"? How can we encourage fellow believers in this way?

_____

_____

_____

One word that can aptly encompass the attitude of encouragement is a heart full of
hope. To meet your spouse's need for encouragement requires that you provide him
or her with hope. Hope means that you believe in your spouse and you will not give
up on him or her no matter how long it takes. To give this kind of hope means that
you receive hope from God. He is the ultimate source and supplier of hope.

Every one of us needs hope. Life is full of opportunities to lose hope, but if we
have even one person who believes in us and does not give up on us, we can overcome just about anything. This is what you can give to your spouse. In fact, no one
can encourage your spouse like you can. Encouragement is giving your spouse the
inspiration to press on through the daily routine of life.

We usually use the word "hope" for an unknown—something in the future that
we want to happen but have no way of knowing if it will. The Bible uses the word
"hope," however, to describe certainty. Consider the certainty of the hope described
in the verses.

> So I pray that God, who gives you hope, will keep you happy and full of
> peace as you believe in him. May you overflow with hope through the
> power of the Holy Spirit. (Romans 15:13)

6. What effect would "overflowing with hope" have on the people around us (and
   especially on our spouse)?

_____

_____

_____

7. We can become better encouragers for our spouse as we reflect upon and consider how God has encouraged you over the years. How has he shown you hope in difficult times?

_____

_____

_____

As with other similar love needs, men and women often need encouragement in different ways:

Men, this is what your wife needs to hear, see, and feel from you:
"You are my one and only! I will always be here for you!"

Women, this is what your husband needs to see, her, and feel from you.
"I am cheering you on! I believe in you! You can do it!"

Attitudes that help with meeting our spouse's need for encouragement include

● **empathy**—the ability to understand what your spouse is feeling;
● **support**—the offer of hope, the cheering on;
● **courage**—to stick it out in the foxhole when the battle is fierce;

8. How can having **empathy** for your spouse help when you want to give encouragement?

_____

_____

_____

_____

9. How does the way of offering **support** differ between men and women?

_____

_____

_____

_____

10. What part does **courage** play in offering encouragement?

_____

_____

_____

SHARING AS A COUPLE

For this section, you and your spouse need to work together in a semiprivate spot in the room to answer the following questions.

11. Together share you answers to questions 8, 9, and 10. Discuss how you can show empathy, offer support, and give courage to your spouse. Take notes below.

_____

_____

_____

PREPARING FOR THE WEEK

During the coming week, you will study the love need of spiritual connection. Remember to do the three days of homework immediately following this lesson. This will include reading chapters 6 and 9 of The Five Love Needs of Men and Women.

This could indeed be a very touchy topic to get into this week. Husbands, if you've not been a strong spiritual leader, don't approach this week with fear and trembling. Instead, open your heart to seek God. He will use your personality and gifts to make you into the perfect leader for your family. It doesn't have to happen overnight; just be open to God and the steps he wants you to take.

Wives, perhaps you're thinking, "Finally! Maybe he'll get his act together and start leading!" I urge you not to do that. Don't nag. Sit back and listen to your husband's concerns. Resist taking the reins away from him (and if you have already been doing so, let him know that you will let him take back over wherever he feels comfortable). Remember what you've learned so far about unconditional love and friendship. Let these be your guides.

Our spiritual lives are very personal. Most important, encourage each other to grow spiritually on a personal level. That will have its own rewards!

End the meeting in prayer.

Week Six—Day One

MY PERSONAL REFLECTION: UNDERSTANDING SPIRITUAL CONNECTION

During the week, read chapters 6 and 9 in *The Five Love Needs of Men and Women*. In chapter 6, Barb talks to husbands about how their wives feel the need for spiritual connection; in chapter 9, Gary talks to wives about how their husbands feel the need for spiritual connection. It will be helpful for both of you to read both chapters.

Because spiritual growth is first of all very personal, let's look at this on a personal level.

1. Overall, when you think about your relationship with God, how do you feel about it? Check a statement below that best describes how you feel, or write your own.

    ❏ I feel that God and I are really close friends, and I am excited about my Christian life.

    ❏ I am not "on fire" for God right now, but I feel okay about my relationship with him.

    ❏ I really have not spent enough time with God in the last few months to know how I am doing in my relationship with him.

    ❏ I feel that God and I are at odds right now.

    ❏ _____

Regardless of your answer to the above question, take a few minutes to talk to God. And then quietly listen to his words to you. The following verses may be helpful for meditation.

> For I know the plans I have for you . . . . They are plans for good and not or disaster, to give you a future and a hope. (Jeremiah 29:11)

I will give you a new heart with new and right desires, and I will put a new spirit in you. I will take out your stony heart of sin and give you a new, obedient heart. (Ezekiel 36:26)

His son said to him, "Father, I have sinned against both heaven and you, and I am no longer worthy of being called your son." But his father said to the servants, "Quick! Bring the finest robe in the house and put it on him. Get a ring for his finger, and sandals for his feet. And kill the calf we have been fattening in the pen. We must celebrate with a feast, for this son of mine was dead and has now returned to life. He was lost, but now he is found." So the party began. (Luke 15:21-24)

"Come now, let us argue this out," says the Lord. "No matter how deep the stain of your sins, I can remove it. I can make you as clean as freshly fallen snow. Even if you are stained as red as crimson, I can make you as white as wool." (Isaiah 1:18)

Answer me when I call, O God who declares me innocent. Take away my distress. Have mercy on me and hear my prayer. . . . You can be sure of this: The Lord has set apart the godly for himself. The Lord will answer when I call to him. (Psalm 4:1-3)

What do you feel God is saying to you?

_____

_____

_____

2. What type of spiritual connection would you like to have with your spouse? Select from the list below, or add your own.

❑ Pray together.
❑ Join a Bible study.
❑ Share with each other how God is working in our lives.
❑ Go to church together.
❑ Serve in a ministry together.
❑ Read the Bible together.
❑ Join a small group in our church.
❑ Share spiritual struggles.
❑ Attend a marriage retreat together.
❑ _____

You may have reservations about trying to connect spiritually with your spouse. Perhaps you have tried in the past to study the Bible or pray with him or her, and these were not pleasant experiences. Maybe you feel intimidated by your spouse's level of maturity and growth. Or, it could be that your obstacles are simply your busy schedules.

Take some time now to consider what you see as potential obstacles to connecting spiritually with your spouse. Be prepared to share these with your spouse during your interaction together later this week.

LEARNING TO SERVE THROUGH SPIRITUAL CONNECTION

Have you ever thought about how badly your spouse needs to be a part of your relationship with God? That is, your spouse wants to grow closer to God with you. Your spouse wants to fellowship with you. This need for fellowship is the most basic, God-given need in a Christian, and it applies to a marriage as well. But spiritual connection is more than just going to church together. It includes a lifestyle that draws your spouse into your daily experiences with God. It means that your spouse is an instrument in God's hands to bring you closer to himself.

3. If you feel that you need to make some improvements/changes in your own spiritual life in order to strengthen it, what are you going to do? (Be specific. If you need to have a quiet time, say, "I am going to spend ten minutes a day reading God's Word right before I go to bed.")

_____

_____

_____

_____

4. What areas of spiritual strength do you see in your spouse?

_____

_____

_____

_____

5. In what area(s) do you think your spouse might be able to use some encouragement?

_____

_____

_____

End this time of reflection by making the following prayer your own.

Dear Lord, I want to grow closer to you. I need to grow in some ways, deepen in others. Work in my heart—unfreeze it, prepare it, make me take more initiative or be less prideful. Show me how I can make that spiritual connection with my spouse so that, together, we can be lights for you. Amen.

Week Six—Day Two

COUPLE INTERACTION:
SERVING MY SPOUSE
WITH SPIRITUAL CONNECTION

You will need to set aside about thirty minutes to complete this exercise with your spouse. Be sure you have selected a place where you will not be interrupted (turn off the phones and pagers, and find a location that will allow you to comfortably share with each other).

This time is intended to help you:

- understand how you can be part of God's plan of meeting your spouse's need for spiritual connection;
- discover a way to practice meeting this need for your spouse;
- plan a time later this week to focus on meeting this need for your spouse.

How Does My Spouse Experience Spiritual Connection?
Take turns sharing with each other how you completed your Personal Reflection questions regarding what you would like to see the two of you do together.

Right now my spouse is feeling

_____

_____

_____

In order to connect spiritually, my spouse would like us to

_____

_____

_____

TALKING IT OVER

Spiritual connection may not come naturally to you. If you're normally a very quiet person who doesn't readily share thoughts, opening up about your relationship with God can be very intimidating. Don't worry. Take into account each other's personalities and don't push beyond the limits. Also make the effort to understand your spouse's needs and be willing to step out of your comfort zone. Take these into account with each other.

Go back to the exercise "Learning to Serve through Spiritual Connection" in the previous day's assignment. Share your answers to question 4 regarding the strengths you see in your spouse.

My spouse sees these spiritual strengths in me:

_____

_____

_____

My spouse would like to encourage me in the following area(s):

_____

_____

_____

What fresh insight did you gain about meeting your spouse's need for spiritual connection? Share that insight with your spouse, and express that you want to connect spiritually.

_____

_____

_____

Pray this prayer together:

> Dear loving Father, we want to connect spiritually. We want to share our relationship with you with each other. Deepen and strengthen our personal walks with you. Help us to set aside time for you personally so that we can grow closer to you. Then help us to share with each other in the areas that we so desire. Overcome our fears, help us in our weaknesses, guide us as we seek to honor you in this way. In Jesus' name, amen.

Week Six—Day Three

MY ASSIGNMENT:
PRACTICING SPIRITUAL CONNECTION

You have two assignments this week:

1. Read chapters 6 and 9 of *The Five Love Needs of Men and Women*.

    Have you completed that assignment yet?

    ❏ Yes   ❏ No   ❏ I've started, but I have more to read.

2. Practice meeting your spouse's need for spiritual connection.

As we've said already, this is going to take time—especially if you and your spouse are treading on new ground. Don't expect vast changes overnight. Take baby steps, work at your own pace as God leads you, and pray for each other. That's really the most important spiritual connection of all!

My Journal

Here is what I did and how it went when I practiced connecting spiritually to my spouse this week.

_____

_____

_____

_____

_____

_____

_____

_____

_____

_____

Here is what I have learned about how I need to meet my spouse's need for spiritual connection.

_____

_____

_____

_____

_____

_____

_____

_____

_____

_____

Group Session Seven

WE ARE ONE IN THE SPIRIT
SPIRITUAL CONNECTION

SETTING THE MOOD

During the week, you and your spouse should have read chapters 6 and 9 of *The Five Love Needs of Men and Women*. Ideally you also made time to work through the homework assignments so that you could discuss how spiritual connection sounds, looks, and feels for each of you.

As the session begins, couples should work together to answer the following questions.

1. In a previous lesson, you wrote down the names of pairs that go together naturally. Now see how many triplets you can list. For example, "bacon, lettuce, and tomato." At the end, include your names, along with God.

    _____, _____, and _____
    _____, _____, and _____
    _____, _____, and _____
    _____, _____, and _____
    _____, _____, and _____
    And us: _____. _____ and _____God_____

2. How much time do you spend reading/studying God's Word each week? Is that about right, or would you like to do more?

    _____
    _____
    _____

3. Discuss what you can do for each other to allow each other quiet time with the Lord. Write your answers below.

My spouse could do for me: _____

I could do for my spouse: _____

Spiritual connection with your spouse begins with your relationship with God. How are you and God doing? Are you still in love with him? Do you think you are growing closer to God? Are you struggling with sin in your life? Are you spending time with God on a regular basis? We wanted you to spend time thinking about these questions this week because, no matter how strong your spiritual connection with your spouse is, you are still responsible for your personal connection with God.

DISCOVERING THE NEED FOR SPIRITUAL CONNECTION

This need is very different from the other love needs in that the Bible assigns us pretty specific roles. While each of us is responsible for our own relationship with God, marriage throws in a curveball. God has ordained men to be the head of their household, to be the spiritual leader of their family, the servant leader. That is a tall order. Men have different personalities and styles of fulfilling (or not fulfilling) this call of God on their lives.

Consider the many possible scenarios. Some men are leading a spiritual astute family. Some men are trying to drag along an unwilling family. Some are unwilling to lead—and might then be facing a wife who desperately wants to be led and so begins to nag her husband to become more spiritual (P.S. It won't work!). Perhaps the wife has taken on the reigns of leadership by default.

Then consider the fact that no man is perfect and no woman is perfect, throw in the ups and downs of life, and you've got a recipe for spiritual upside-down cake!

As difficult as this is, women ranked a spiritual connection with their husbands as their number three love need, and men ranked it as their number five love need. Clearly we want to connect on that deep level. Most of us would say that our most important relationship in life is with our Savior, Jesus Christ. Of course, we want to share that with our spouse. We want to include our spouse in our walk with the Lord.

Spiritual intimacy and connection is the need to experience the love of God with another person.

Gary says to wives:

Your husband, like every Christian husband, needs to be growing spiritually. He needs spiritual connection—with God, with you, and with other believers. If husbands are going to take the Bible seriously, then they know that one of the key dimensions of their spiritual life is the spiritual leadership they must provide. . . . This spiritual responsibility weighs heavily on your husband when he recognizes that you and your children are relying on him to lead. Add to that the fact that he knows that God is going to hold him accountable for the way he carries out that mandate. . . . You are a major part of the equation in keeping your marriage spiritually on track. . . . Pray faithfully for your husband.
(pages 175, 176, 179, 192)

Barb says to husbands:

God is asking a lot of you! . . . Your wife longs to experience the fulfillment that comes from knowing you love God and are willing to serve him by being an effective husband and father. So as you strengthen your relationship with God and take on your God-given roles in the home, you will help her strengthen her relationship with God and with you. . . . Don't leave your wife hurting and yearning to experience spiritual intimacy, longing for what could have been. Today's a new day. Begin it by committing yourself to developing a spiritual closeness with your wife—your very best friend.
(pages 121, 141)

THE HEART ATTITUDE OF SPIRITUAL CONNECTION

Read the following verses from the apostle Paul's letter to the Colossians.

> Let the words of Christ, in all their richness, live in your hearts and make you wise. Use his words to teach and counsel each other. Sing psalms and hymns and spiritual songs to God with thankful hearts. And whatever you do or say, let it be as a representative of the Lord Jesus, all the while giving thanks through him to God the Father. You wives must submit to your husbands, as is fitting for those who belong to the Lord. And you husbands must love your wives and never treat them harshly. . . . Devote yourselves to prayer with an alert mind and a thankful heart. (Colossians 3:16-19; 4:2)

4. Spiritual connection with your spouse begins with your personal relationship with God. What does Paul say about how we should approach God's Word?

_____

_____

_____

_____

5. What should be your attitude toward your spouse?

_____

_____

_____

6. How should you live your daily life?

_____

_____

_____

7. Discuss as a group some concerns about and obstacles to spiritual connection that are listed below. Don't feel that you have to share about your own particular concerns; this is simply a time to draw on the group for suggestions in how to handle various situations that can cause us to shy away from spiritual connection. Under each concern or obstacle, write various answers that the group offers to help overcome them:

My spouse and I are just so busy; we can't find the time.

_____

_____

_____

I really have not spent enough time with God in the last few months to know how I am doing in my relationship with him.

_____

_____

_____

I feel that God and I are at odds right now.

_____

_____

_____

I feel that I do not pray very well.

_____

_____

_____

My spouse and I have tried to study and pray together before, but we didn't stick with it.

_____

_____

_____

I feel spiritually empty right now.

_____

_____

_____

My spouse knows God's Word so much better that I feel intimidated.

_____

_____

_____

I don't have a personal quiet time, so I don't want to try to do it together.

_____

_____

_____

My spouse and I are both new Christians and don't know what to do.

_____

_____

_____

Our ideas are so different that we always end up in an argument.

_____

_____

_____

My spouse is much more mature in the faith, and I feel intimidated.

_____

_____

_____

_____

Why does it matter that we connect spiritually with our spouse? Well, God's plan is for us to connect with all believers. You see, as personal as is our spiritual relationship with God, we are also part of a community. Like a coal in a fire, if we are separated from the other coals, we quickly cool off and burn out. But when we stay grouped together, we can keep the fire going. Being a Christian means being part of a family, with God as our Father. God knows that we need each other. We can't go it alone.

In our marriages, then, God knows that a spiritual connection is vital as we face the daily challenges, raise our children, make our decisions, plan our futures. We can't do it without him; we shouldn't do it without each other. Consider how the verses below apply to your spiritual connection with your spouse. Write that description on the lines following each verse.

> A person standing alone can be attacked and defeated, but two can stand back-to-back and conquer. Three are even better, for a triple-braided cord is not easily broken. (Ecclesiastes 4:12)

_____

_____

_____

> "Yes, I am the vine; you are the branches. Those who remain in me, and I in them, will produce much fruit. For apart from me you can do nothing." (John 15:5)

_____

_____

_____

PREPARING FOR THE WEEK

During this week, you will finish the book The Five Love Needs of Men and Women *by reading chapters 11 and 12. The closing chapters help to tie up the thoughts from all that you've covered over the last five weeks. This time, Gary talks to husbands after having read Barb's advice, and he adds some of his own. Likewise, Barb talks to wives after having read the five chapters of Gary's advice, and pulls together final thoughts as well.*

The homework this week will help you think through all that you've learned. You might feel a bit overwhelmed at all that you've taken in during the last seven weeks. Don't be discouraged. Enjoy this week of review—and realize that you've got a lifetime together to practice!

End the meeting in prayer.

Week Seven—Day One

MY PERSONAL REFLECTION:
UNDERSTANDING
THE NEXT STEPS

During the week, read chapters 11 and 12 in *The Five Love Needs of Men and Women*. In chapter 11, Gary talks to husbands and does a wrap-up of all that has been learned during these last seven weeks; in chapter 12, Barb talks to wives and does the same thing. It will be helpful for both of you to read both chapters.

If you haven't already felt a bit overwhelmed by all you've learned these past weeks, you might be feeling so now. It may feel as if there's just too much to take in. Fortunately, you don't have to spend the last session taking a test to see how much you've improved in meeting all five of your spouse's love needs. You don't need to do an oral report and get straight A's in every area.

What you need to do, instead, is sit back quietly and get a perspective on all that you've learned. You need to think about your marriage, your spouse, your current situation in life, and what you can do—today—to take the next step on the road to a healthy, long-lasting, loving marriage.

Following are two sections—one for husbands to do, and one for wives to do. Complete the appropriate section.

For husbands:

> **Gary says to the men:**
> *Now that you've received some insights from Barb. . . . Here are a few options:*
> *1. Incorporate all the changes tomorrow.*
> *2. Think it's too much work and not do anything. (After all, you're better than most guys you know.)*
> *3. Pick two or three things to work on in the next few months.*

If you picked #1, call my office for an appointment. You're going to need counseling to deal with the overwhelming sense of anxiety you just bit off. If you picked #2, then you are more hard-hearted and hardheaded than I could imagine. As you can probably tell, I recommend #3 . . .

(pages 211–212)

Following are a few questions Gary challenges you to put before God as you move from the learning stage to the application stage of meeting your wife's love needs and pursuing a great marriage. Ask God:

1. How do you want me to show my unconditional love by serving my wife more fully?

    _____

    _____

    _____

2. How do you want me to step outside of my own selfishness and learn how to listen—really listen—to my wife's heart as she expresses her emotions and needs?

    _____

    _____

    _____

3. What do you want me to put down—my golf clubs, fishing rod, bowling ball, or remote control—in order to step into her world, ministering to her as her friend as well as husband, lover, and partner?

    _____

    _____

    _____

4. How about encouragement? In what ways do I need to face the reality that my negative and neutral comments might outweigh the affirming ones I give my wife each day?

    _____

    _____

    _____

5. Father, how shall I minister to my wife's spirit? Maybe taking her hand in bed tonight to pray together would be a place to start. How about if I initiate reading

your Word with her and perhaps taking a walk together to share what we are learning from you?

_____

_____

_____

For wives:

Barb says to the women:

Whether it's my marriage or yours, great marriages are often forged through trials. In your particular season of marriage, your life may be out of control. James 1:2-4, however, tells us, "Dear brothers and sisters, whenever trouble comes your way, let it be an opportunity for joy". . . . So don't look at trials as an enemy. . . . But what of the normal times of marriage? If your marriage is void of major trial at this point in life, how can you work on getting your relationship ready to withstand the minor irritations or "the test" that may still be off in the future?
(pages 226-227)

Following are a few questions Barb challenges you to put before God as you move from the learning stage to the application stage of meeting your husband's love needs and pursuing a great marriage. Ask God:

1. How do you want me to show my unconditional love for my husband? How can I be more tender, more a student of my husband?

    _____

    _____

    _____

2. How do you want me to be more sensitive to his sexual needs and desires?

    _____

    _____

    _____

    _____

3. How do you want me to step into his world and enjoy him as my best friend?

    _____

    _____

    _____

4. How about encouragement? Does my husband hear enough praise from me, or am I negative and nagging? Father, what should I do to improve?

_____

_____

_____

5. How can I help him to be the spiritual leader without nagging or putting unfair expectations on him? What should I do or not do?

_____

_____

_____

LEARNING TO SERVE THROUGH MEETING THE LOVE NEEDS
Gary's suggestion to the men, quoted above, is important for both husbands and wives to take to heart. You won't be able to incorporate all that you've learned these last seven weeks all at once. But you don't want to sit back and decide not to try to improve your marriage at all. Instead, let's go somewhere in the middle. Let's pick two or three things to work on in the next few months.

6. Considering all I've learned in the last few weeks, I think I could use the most improvement in meeting my spouse's love needs in the following two areas:

_____

_____

End this time of reflection by making the following prayer your own.

Dear Lord, thank you for all I've learned over the past seven weeks. I love my husband [wife], Lord, and I want to help make our marriage the very best it can be. I want to learn how better to meet my spouse's love needs. Give me wisdom to know where I should begin—and give me the strength and courage to keep it up. Amen.

Week Seven—Day Two

COUPLE INTERACTION:
SERVING MY SPOUSE THROUGH THE LOVE NEEDS

You will need to set aside about thirty minutes to complete this exercise with your spouse. Be sure you have selected a place where you will not be interrupted (turn off the phones and pagers, and find a location that will allow you to comfortably share with each other).

This time is intended to help you:

- understand what you need to do in the various areas of the love needs to help to meet your spouse's needs;
- discover two places to begin working on meeting your spouse's love needs.

WHERE DO WE BEGIN?
Take turns sharing with each other how you completed your five Personal Reflection questions.

My spouse wants to show unconditional love by

_____

_____

_____

My spouse wants to help meet my emotional/physical needs by

_____

_____

_____

My spouse wants to be a better friend by

_____

_____

_____

My spouse desires to encourage me by

_____

_____

_____

My spouse wants to make a spiritual connection by

_____

_____

_____

TALKING IT OVER

Go back to the exercise "Learning to Serve through Meeting the Love Needs" in the previous day's assignment. Share your two answers to question 7 regarding the areas where you would like to begin.

My spouse is going to begin working on:

_____

_____

_____

Pray this prayer together:

> Dear loving Father, we want to meet each other's love needs, but we know we have a long way to go. We also know that in our own strength, we can't even begin. Help us, Lord, with your strength through your Holy Spirit to recognize and meet each other's love needs. In Jesus' name, amen.

Week Seven—Day Three

MY ASSIGNMENT:
PRACTICE MAKES PERFECT!

You have two assignments this week:

1. Read chapters 11 and 12 of *The Five Love Needs of Men and Women*.

    Have you completed that assignment yet?

    ❑ Yes   ❑ No   ❑ I've started, but I have more to read.

2. Practice working on the two areas you've suggested as places where you want to begin.

An ancient adage says that the journey of a thousand miles begins with a single step. You may have thousands of miles to go before you think your marriage can be all you want it to be. But going hand in hand, you can take those steps together.

My Journal

Here is what I did and how it went when I began working on the specific areas I pinpointed in meeting my spouse's love needs.

_____

_____

_____

_____

_____

Group Session Eight

BEGIN THE JOURNEY— TOGETHER

SETTING THE MOOD

During the week, you and your spouse should have read chapters 11 and 12 of *The Five Love Needs of Men and Women.* Ideally you also made time to work through the homework assignments.

As the session begins, couples should work together to answer the following questions.

1. The best thing about this course to me has been

   _____

   _____

   _____

2. The most surprising thing I learned about my spouse was

   _____

   _____

   _____

DISCOVERING THE NEED TO KEEP GROWING

You did it! You've worked for seven weeks on meeting each other's love needs. But where do you go from here? You've taken in a lot of information. Now what? Let's divide into groups of men and women, and we'll discuss the next steps. Men, do the section for you below; women, do your section, which is farther down.

A FINAL WORD TO THE MEN

Men, read the following quotes from Gary, and work together to answer the accompanying questions.

Gary's final word to men:
When I attend a conference, read a book, or try to assimilate some change in my life, the first thing I do is step back and try to get a clear perspective. Second, I pray and ask God what he wants me to learn from what I have just studied. Perspective and God. Those are the two things I love to seek out. Sounds like a good place to start, doesn't' it? . . . Finding direction is the best first move. But remember, you can't do it all at once. You have to start somewhere.
(page 212)

Unconditional love
Gary says that unconditional love is all about "servant leadership" (page 213). What have you learned about servant leadership that you can incorporate in your marriage?

_____

_____

_____

Emotional intimacy
Gary says that this boils down to stoking your wife's emotional fires and staying away from campsites not your own (page 217). How can you commit to both of these in your marriage?

_____

_____

_____

Spiritual connection
Gary says "you will have a great marriage when you honor your wife" (page 217). How will you commit to doing that?

_____

_____

_____

Encouragement

"You are called to be your wife's number one encourager," says Gary (page 219). In what ways can husbands encourage their wives?

_____

_____

_____

Friendship

How are you going to step into your wife's world and be her best friend?

_____

_____

_____

A FINAL WORD TO THE WOMEN

Women, read the following quote from Barb and work together to answer the accompanying questions.

Barb's final word to women:

Meeting any or all of your husband's love needs also means not trying to do it under your own power. It can't be done. I've discovered four things I can do to make sure it's God's power doing the work, not mine. I call them my "four Ps." They aren't radically different from anything you've heard before, but they work!

Personal, daily time reading the Word. . . . *Find a place where you can go to hide away from it all and spend time with God and his Word. Then apply what the Scriptures are teaching you by responding to your husband in a godly way.*

Prayer. *Don't miss a day. . . . If you want to truly meet your husband's love needs and have a great marriage, then you must humble yourself and turn toward the infinite wisdom of a powerful God. Begin every prayer with words of thanksgiving and praise for what he has done in your life.*

Partner with a friend. *When I'm wading through high waters, I am quick to call my prayer partners. . . . This partnership with other women of kindred hearts really works!*

Past provision of God. *When discouragement stabs you out of the dark, thank God for how he has worked in the past. Neither you nor I know what the future holds, but we know the One who does. He promises to never leave us or forsake us. And remember, he is the best promise keeper. . . .*

A great marriage isn't a dream; it's a choice. Meeting your husband's love needs isn't an option; it's a must!

(pages 232-233, 234)

Unconditional love

Barb wants you to understand that your husband needs to feel safe enough with you to take off his mask and be transparent (page 227). How can you tenderly show your husband your unconditional love?

_____

_____

_____

Physical intimacy

Barb says, "Don't forget that most men find a great deal of their masculinity in their sexuality" (page 229). How can you be a better partner in this area?

_____

_____

_____

Friendship

Barb says to satisfy your husband's friendship needs by joining him in his favorite activities (page 231). How can you do that?

_____

_____

_____

Encouragement

"He can never hear enough praise from you," says Barb about husbands (page 231). How will you be a better cheerleader for your husband?

_____

_____

_____

Spiritual connection

How will you let God work in your husband's life?

_____

_____

_____

Which of the four "Ps" from Barb's quote above do you think will be most helpful to you as you seek to fulfill your commitment to meeting your husband's love needs?

_____

_____

_____

IN CLOSING

As you read in chapter 11, Gary quoted an e-mail that he received from a man who witnessed a loving marriage. The author of the e-mail had commented to the man: "I hope my marriage is still that passionate after twelve years!"

To which the gentleman replied, "Don't hope, friend. Decide!"

It's up to you now. Decide *to make your marriage the best it can be!*

Ask each couple to hold hands. End the session in prayer.

Serving Love

LEADER NOTES

We are so thankful for you! Your willingness to partner with us in strengthening America's marriages means that more and more families can be spared the ordeal of divorce. We are so excited about getting this message into as many marriages as possible across this country. We have called our campaign Divorce-Proofing America's Marriages, and the first book, *Divorce-Proof Your Marriage,* describes the six key kinds of love that every marriage needs in order to stay strong and healthy. One of those kinds of loves is serving love, and that is the focus of our book *The Five Love Needs of Men and Women* and this companion workbook called *Serving Love.*

We hope that you're taking on the leadership of your group to study serving love because you're excited—you also want to spread this message to as many people as you can! You see, in order to make these sessions work, you, the leader, need to be enthusiastic about the topic. You're going to need to motivate the married couples in your group to read the book and do their homework assignments. These are key. The homework is not a requirement, but stress to the couples that they will get so much more out of this time if they are willing to *make* the time to do these assignments during the week.

While you can work your way through each chapter along with the group without much extra assistance, these Leader Notes will provide some transition statements and instructions where needed.

1. Order and distribute the following books to the couples at the first session:
    ● One copy of the book *The Five Love Needs of Men and Women* for **every couple** attending.
    ● One *Serving Love* workbook for **every person** attending.

2. Contact all attendees a few days prior to the first session to remind them of the time and meeting location, and ask them to arrive at least ten minutes before the session starts.

3. You will lead each session by reading the workbook lesson in its entirety. The participants will follow along in their workbooks and complete the exercises as you instruct them. Use the additional comments in these Leader Notes as you have the time.

4. Scripture passages are provided at appropriate times in the workbook. All passages are from the New Living Translation published by Tyndale House Publishers. This will make it easier for everyone to follow along from the same translation. You can have someone in the group read these passages, or you can read them to the group.

5. Begin each session with prayer. This entire study assumes that God has brought this group together. Consider the following when you pray with the group:
    ● We recognize that God brought every person to this study for a reason.
    ● We are excited to discover new things about ourselves and our spouses.
    ● We expect God to use his Holy Spirit to teach us how to better meet our spouses' love needs.
    ● We give God the glory for the ways he will make our marriages better as we submit to his plan for us.

6. Consider how to help with child care. Perhaps your church youth group can help with this.

7. Room preparation:
    ● Provide name tags, and ask attendees to prepare the tags as they arrive.
    ● Have a list of all attendees who signed up. Ask everyone to verify that his or her name is on the class sheet. Have someone at a table near the entrance to welcome each couple.
    ● If you are charging each couple for the books and workbooks, have someone at the table to collect the money for the books that have been distributed.
    ● Make sure you have adequate seating for everyone.

8. A note about the structure of this eight-week study: The first session is designed to introduce the couples to the five love needs. It will briefly review the five types of love that will be covered. Then, there are three days of homework during which couples will consider the love need that will be discussed in the next

group session. Encourage your group members to make an effort to do their homework as they will come better prepared for the group sessions.

9. Pray for your group members each week. Ask God to intervene with his Spirit to empower each couple to understand and meet each other's needs.

Leader Notes: Group Session One

WHAT ARE YOUR LOVE NEEDS?

LESSON PURPOSE

- To help married couples understand the five basic love needs men and women have in their marriages.
- To guide married couples to consider their own love needs.

LESSON PLAN

Open in prayer.

Introduction

Spend a few minutes briefly touching on the material contained in the "Introduction—How to Use This Book" section of this workbook. Discuss the focus and goals of this course as described in the introduction, and make sure everyone understands the three days of homework that each couple is to complete during the week between each group session.

Setting the Mood

As a group, discuss questions 1 and 2. Read aloud the special note from Gary and Barb at the beginning of this workbook.

Discovering the Need

Ask someone to read aloud the quote from Gary and Barb. Then answer questions 3 and 4. Read aloud the two paragraphs after question 4. Then answer questions 5 and 6.

Transition:

"Is it being selfish to want our love needs met? Has God given us various needs he wants to meet in our spouse for the purpose of deepening our relationships with each other? Let's identify five biblically based love needs and define them. Gary and Barb did a study of over seven hundred couples, presenting them with a list of twenty needs and asking them to rank, in order of importance, what they needed from their spouse. This chart represents their findings. You can find the list of twenty needs in appendix B. I would encourage you and your spouse to go ahead and work through the list of twenty. For purposes of this study, we are working with the top five that were discovered in that study. It is interesting to note that men and women ranked very similar love needs as their top five—just in slightly different order. We will discover that *the way* those needs are filled, however, differs between men and women."

Read the paragraph following question 6 and the chart of the five love needs of men and women. As a group, work on question 7. You are to answer for each love need: (1) how you would define it; (2) how it might show itself in marriage; and (3) why you think meeting that love need is important in marriage. Some definitions of each love need are noted below. You can read these aloud to the group prior to having them fill in the blanks.

UNCONDITIONAL LOVE

This means that you will look past your spouse's faults and failures and love your spouse completely, even when he/she fails you. Do you think your spouse needs to be loved in this way? The answer is yes, isn't it? And we can say that God made our spouses with this need. Therefore, this is a legitimate need that we can meet.

INTIMACY (SEXUAL [MEN]/EMOTIONAL [WOMEN])

We are created to have an intimate relationship with Christ through his Spirit. He encourages us. He comforts us. Our hearts are tender and sympathetic to others because of what Christ has done in us. God made your spouse to need all of these things from you. One word captures the essence of applying these principles in marriage: Intimacy. God created our spouse to need intimacy.

SPIRITUAL INTIMACY

Growth encourages growth. If you are growing spiritually, you will encourage those around you to grow spiritually. Gary and Barb Rosberg have discovered through their research that growing together spiritually is one of the key ingredients for a couple who want a vibrant marriage. These verses identify a God-given need in our spouse: it is the need for spiritual connection. This means that each of us will make our spouse's spiritual growth a priority. A key to doing this is wrapped up in the word *share*. This means we talk about spiritual issues and we participate in spiritual activities with each other.

ENCOURAGEMENT/AFFIRMATION

This is not just an ordinary kind of encouragement. If we were to describe it in our culture today, we would think of the athletes on the field who are "emotionally charged" by the cheering fans. Their cheering provokes and encourages the athletes to excel and to accomplish more because of the encouragement they receive. Imagine what it would mean to your spouse if you became his or her biggest fan! Have you ever considered that your spouse needs you above all others to come alongside and cheer him or her on through the good as well as the bad times? This course will help you learn how to do just that!

COMPANIONSHIP

I am sure we all agree that we need friends. But have you ever considered that your spouse needs to be your friend? Research consistently proves that those marriages that last and thrive do so because the husband and wife are friends. In fact, many researchers will argue that the when you find strong marriages, you will find a husband and wife who are best friends. Indeed, that is one goal of this course. To help you become your spouse's best friend.

Complete question 8 as a group.

Sharing as a Couple

Have the couples work together by moving into semiprivate locations in the room. The questions are for them to work on together; however, they are not so private that it would be embarrassing to discuss in semiprivacy. Allow the couples a few minutes to determine each other's top five love needs based on the five that will be studied in this course.

Bring the group back together.

Preparing for the Week

Read aloud the ground rules for the session and make sure everyone understands. It should be made very clear that this is a very safe place and anything shared is to remain confidential. In addition, make the rule that spouses are not allowed to talk negatively about each other in front of the group. We're focusing on the positive here! If they need to have a discussion, there is plenty of opportunity provided in the homework assignments.

Remind the couples of the three days of homework that will prepare them for the discussion in the next session on unconditional love.

End the meeting in prayer.

Leader Notes: Group Session Two

LOVE THAT IS
"FOR BETTER OR FOR WORSE"
UNCONDITIONAL LOVE

LESSON PURPOSE

- To discuss in depth the importance of unconditional love in marriage.
- To guide married couples to consider how to show unconditional love to each other.

LESSON PLAN

Open in prayer.

Setting the Mood
Have each couple work together to discuss and answer questions 1 and 2.

Transition:
> *Bring to class some newspaper or magazine ads that promise great deals but have lots of disclaimers and fine print at the bottom of the page. Read the ad, then read the disclaimers—in a fast voice, like the radio announcers.*

"What if everyone came into marriage making the big promises, like these advertisements, but also having lots of disclaimers?"

Read the paragraphs in the workbook.

"It is great to be on the receiving end of unconditional love, isn't it? Listen to how Gary explains it in their book:

Gary says:

When my wife needs my unconditional love, it simply means that she needs me to love her and receive her no matter what. For richer or for poorer. In sickness and in health. You remember the vows. Unconditional love is the commitment that says:"I will stay with you no matter what. I will always love you. I will affirm you and support you."Acceptance means,"I will receive you even in the midst of tough times."

Barb and I have found that our love for each other is glorious in the good times—the vacations on the beach, the memory-making experiences with the kids, the times of deep intimacy together with Jesus Christ. It's easy to love in the good times. But when our marriage comes under intense testing, we need unconditional *love. Love that won't quit.We need to know we are accepted even when we come up short, even when we can't see beyond our own pain and failures.*

(pages 15–16)

"During this last week you have had opportunities to talk about how you need to demonstrate this kind of love for each other. And while we want to love others this way, sometimes it is difficult."

Discovering the Need for Unconditional Love
Read the paragraphs and the definition of unconditional love. Have a man read what Gary says to wives, then have a woman read what Barb says to husbands.

THE HEART ATTITUDE OF UNCONDITIONAL LOVE
Ask someone to read the verses from Romans 6, and then work together to answer question 3.

Read the intervening paragraphs, then answer question 4.

Work your way through question 5 by discussing the nine characteristics found in 1 Corinthians 13:4-5. Have the group explain why they think each attitude is important in expressing unconditional love. The nine characteristics are patient, kind, not jealous, not boastful, not proud, not rude, not demanding one's own way, not irritable, and keeps no record of wrongs.

Transition:
"These nine characteristics can be condensed into four basic attitudes. These four attitudes can be summarized by the word *grace*. Grace is loving another with the understanding that God loves me in spite of my sin and accepts me without reservation. In other words, when I show grace, I love as God loves me."

Discuss question 6.

Have each person individually rate himself/herself on the scales in question 7.

Sharing as a Couple
Have the couples work together by moving into semiprivate locations in the room. Allow the couples a few minutes to work together and answer questions 8, 9, and 10.

Preparing for the Week
Explain the homework assignment and read the closing paragraphs.

End the meeting in prayer.

Leader Notes: Group Session Three

THE TWO SHALL BE ONE MEN AND INTIMACY

LESSON PURPOSE

- To discuss in depth how men view intimacy in marriage.
- To guide married couples to consider how to meet each other's need for intimacy—in particular, sexual intimacy.

LESSON PLAN

Open in prayer.

Setting the Mood
Have couples work together to answer questions 1 and 2. Make sure the spouses fill in their names at the end of the list.

Transition:
"Intimacy is vital to every marriage, but as we learned last week (and perhaps as you learned during this intervening week), men and women define intimacy very differently. Because of that difference, we will be focusing today on how men view intimacy; next week we'll look at how women view intimacy."

Read the paragraphs.

Discovering the Need for Physical Intimacy
Read aloud the material and the definition of intimacy. Consider how men and women view intimacy so differently. Then read the quote from Gary.

The Heart Attitude of Physical Intimacy

These verses describe God's blessing on the sexual union of husbands and wives. Read each verse, and then answer questions 3 through 7 as a group.

> *It is important that you as a leader be sensitive to the needs in your group. You may or may not know of extreme difficulties in some marriages due to baggage from the past in the form of some kind of abuse. Encourage the members of your class that because physical intimacy is so important (it is a legitimate love need), they need to work together to deal with such unresolved issues. They should find counsel through a pastor or Christian counselor if needed.*

Read aloud the paragraph, and then divide the group into two smaller groups—one of men and one of women. Have them answer the question in their small groups.

Sharing as a Couple

After they have completed the exercise in their two small groups, divide again into couples and have the couples work together by moving into semiprivate locations in the room. Allow them a few minutes to work together and answer questions 8 and 9.

Preparing for the Week

Explain the homework assignment and read the closing paragraphs.

End the meeting in prayer.

Leader Notes: Group Session Four

JUST TALK TO ME
WOMEN AND INTIMACY

LESSON PURPOSE

- To discuss in depth how women view intimacy in marriage.
- To guide married couples to consider how to meet each other's need for intimacy—in particular, emotional intimacy.

LESSON PLAN

Open in prayer.

Setting the Mood
Have the couples work together on questions 1 and 2.

Transition:
"Last week we talked about how men view intimacy and we discussed the importance of that sexual relationship. Today we're going to focus on how women view intimacy."

Discovering the Need for Emotional Intimacy
Read aloud the material, and review the definition of intimacy. Then read the quote from Barb.

THE HEART ATTITUDE OF EMOTIONAL INTIMACY
Have someone read the verses from Philippians as printed in the workbook. Then work as a group to answer questions 3 through 6.

Transition:

"We may recognize the need for intimacy, but we discover that it takes work to make the time to have emotional (not to mention sexual) intimacy. Let's discuss some of the obstacles to intimacy and think about ways we can overcome those obstacles."

Work as a group on question 7. As you do, fill in the columns, first listing some of the problems that are obstacles to intimacy (such as not having time, which is already on the list). Then have the group suggest why this is a problem, and finally, give suggestions for ways to overcome that problem.

Divide into groups of men and women, and have each group work to answer question 8.

Sharing as a Couple

Have the couples work together by moving into semiprivate locations in the room. Allow the couples a few minutes to work together and answer questions 9, 10, and 11.

Preparing for the Week

Explain the homework assignment, and read the closing paragraphs.

End the meeting in prayer.

Leader Notes: Group Session Five

DISCOVERING YOUR BEST FRIEND
COMPANIONSHIP

LESSON PURPOSE

- To discuss in depth the importance of companionship in marriage.
- To guide married couples to consider how to be each other's favorite companions.

LESSON PLAN

Open in prayer.

Setting the Mood
Have the couples work together to answer questions 1 through 3.

Transition:
"When you were dating, you couldn't wait to spend time together. And when you couldn't be together, you were on the telephone. You were friends; you wanted to share everything. Sometimes the very familiarity of marriage takes away some of that spark. We need to relight it!"

Read the paragraphs about friendship.

Discovering the Need for Companionship
Read aloud the material and the definition of companionship. Answer question 4 by having the men and women describe what friendship means to them—what they like to do when they get together with their same-sex friends. Write these in the appropriate columns. Then answer question 5.

Read aloud the quotes from Gary and Barb.

THE HEART ATTITUDE OF COMPANIONSHIP
Read each proverb and discuss as a group how King Solomon's words would apply in their friendship with their spouses.

Transition:
"The Bible sure has a lot to say about friendship. And, as we've seen, these words apply to our marriages. All of these verses can be boiled down to three words."

As a group, answer questions 7 through 9. However, in between answering the questions, each individual should rate himself/herself on the scales provided.

Read aloud the paragraph in the workbook.

Sharing as a Couple
Have the couples work together by moving into semiprivate locations in the room. Allow the couples a few minutes to work together and answer question 10.

Preparing for the Week
Explain the homework assignment, and read the closing paragraphs.

End the meeting in prayer.

Leader Notes: Group Session Six

YOUR OWN PRIVATE CHEERING SECTION
ENCOURAGEMENT

LESSON PURPOSE

- To discuss in depth the importance of encouragement and affirmation in marriage.
- To guide married couples to consider how to encourage and affirm each other.

LESSON PLAN

Open in prayer.

Setting the Mood
Give the couples a few minutes to work together to answer questions 1 and 2.

Read aloud the material in the workbook.

> *Find out if there are any former cheerleaders or jocks in the room. Ask if anyone still remembers any cheers. Also ask how those jocks felt about having the cheerleaders and the people in the stands cheering them on. What would have been different if there had been no fans there to watch the game? What about if everyone had booed at them the entire time?*

Transition:
"We love to have people encourage us, but how often do we forget to say those needed words to others? We may *think* it, but just don't get around to saying it. You probably discovered this week that you both need to hear encouraging and affirming words from each other. Let's talk about that some more today."

Discovering the Need for Encouragement

Read aloud the material and the definition of encouragement. Then read the quotes from Gary and Barb.

THE HEART ATTITUDE OF ENCOURAGEMENT

Read the verses and answer questions 3, 4, and 5. Then read the intervening material before moving on to questions 6 and 7.

Read the material that discusses how men like to be encouraged and how women like to be encouraged. You could ask the men and women to share some of their own "favorite phrases" of encouragement that they shared with their spouses during the week.

Note the three attitudes that help in being able to be an encourager. Use questions 8, 9, and 10 to discuss these further.

Transition:

"Encouragement is really easy. Say it with a gift. Say it with words. Say it with a hug or a touch. Say it with a special date out in order to spend time together. Say it in a way that your spouse will hear and get the message: 'I love you. You're the greatest! Thank you for all you do for me.'"

Sharing as a Couple

Have the couples work together by moving into semiprivate locations in the room. Allow the couples a few minutes to work together and answer question 11.

Preparing for the Week

Explain the homework assignment and read the closing paragraphs.

End the meeting in prayer.

WE ARE ONE IN THE SPIRIT
SPIRITUAL CONNECTION

LESSON PURPOSE

- To discuss in depth the importance of spiritual connection in marriage.
- To guide married couples to consider how to make a spiritual connection each other.

LESSON PLAN

Open in prayer.

Setting the Mood
Have couples work together to fill out the triplets in question 1. Then they should also answer questions 2 and 3 together.

Read aloud the paragraphs.

Discovering the Need for Spiritual Connection
Read aloud the material and the definition of spiritual connection. Then read the quotes from Gary and Barb.

The Heart Attitude of Spiritual Connection
Read the passage in Colossians, and work together as a group to answer questions 4 through 6.

There are plenty of obstacles to spiritual connection, and some of these are listed in question 7. Ask the group to read each obstacle and then brainstorm about ways to overcome that obstacle.

Read the material aloud.

Sharing as a Couple
Have the couples work together to answer question 8 by reading the verses and answering them for their own marriages.

Preparing for the Week
We have officially completed the study of the love needs. The final three days of homework and group session provide the opportunity to pull together their thoughts and give a focus to what they want to work on in their marriages.

End the meeting in prayer.

Leader Notes: Group Session Eight

BEGIN THE JOURNEY— TOGETHER

LESSON PURPOSE

- To take the time to think about all they have learned.
- To consider one area they want to begin working on in their marriages in order to begin to meet their spouse's love needs.

LESSON PLAN

Open in prayer.

Setting the Mood
Ask couples to work together on questions 1 and 2.

Discovering the Need to Keep Growing
Read aloud the material. Make two groups—one of men and one of women. Ask someone in each group to read aloud the quotation. Then the groups should work together to answer the questions.

In Closing
Your group has experienced eight weeks of intense study about their marriage relationships. They may indeed feel overwhelmed. Ideally each person will be able to go away from this last session with one area on which to focus as he or she seek to meet love needs. Help them to understand that you have provided them with a "tool box." As they continue to work on their marriages in the days, months, and years ahead, they should remind themselves of the tools they have learned in these eight weeks and use them when needed.

Thank the group for coming and for their diligent work over the last eight weeks. Encourage them to go back and finish any exercises that they may not have completed.

Pray for God's blessings on their marriages and on their families.

APPENDICES

CAMPAIGN RESOURCES FOR DIVORCE-PROOFING AMERICA'S MARRIAGES

Dear friends,

The resources for the Divorce-Proofing America's Marriages campaign are designed *for you*—to help you divorce-proof your marriage. You and your spouse can certainly read and study these books as a couple. But it's only when you meet with a small group that is committed to divorce-proofing their marriages as well that you'll fully experience the power of these ideas. There's power when believers unite in a common cause. There's power when men and women keep each other accountable. To take on this challenge, you must have a group of friends who are encouraging you every step of the way.

There are several ways you can connect to a small group:

- Start your own Divorce-Proofing America's Marriages small group in your church or neighborhood. For workbooks, leader's guides, videos, and other resources for your small group, call 888-ROSBERG (888-767-2374) or visit our Web site at **www.divorceproof.com**.

- Give this information to your pastor or elders at your local church. They may want to host a Divorce-Proofing America's Marriages small group in your church.

- Call America's Family Coaches at 888-ROSBERG (888-767-2374), or e-mail us at afc@afclive.com and we will connect you with people and churches who are interested in Divorce-Proofing America's Marriages.

Yes, together we can launch a nationwide campaign and see countless homes transformed into covenant homes. But beware. If we do not teach these principles to our own children, we risk missing the greatest opportunity of all: to pass our legacy of godly homes to the next generation. Barb and I believe that, *for the sake of the next generation,* there is no more worthy cause. This holy fire must purify our own homes first.

Gary and Barb Rosberg

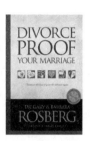

DIVORCE-PROOF YOUR MARRIAGE
ISBN 0-8423-4995-2
Audio CD (3 CDs) ISBN 0-8423-6592-3
Audiocassette (2 cassettes) ISBN 0-8423-6894-9

DISCOVER THE LOVE OF YOUR LIFE ALL OVER AGAIN (workbook)
ISBN 0-8423-7342-X

Your house is weatherproofed. But is your marriage divorce-proofed? In this foundational book of the Divorce-Proofing America's Marriages campaign, Gary and Barb show couples how to keep their marriages safe from the threat of divorce. Divorce doesn't happen suddenly. Over months and years couples can slide from the dream to disappointment and eventually to emotional divorce. However, they can stop the slide by learning to love in six unique ways. Small groups will enjoy the *Discover the Love of Your Life All Over Again* workbook, which includes eight sessions. Together couples will practice healing hurt in their marriages, meeting their spouses' needs, strengthening each other through difficult times, guarding their marriage against threats, celebrating their spouses, and renewing their love for each other day after day. A weekly devotion and assignment will help couples practice what they learn in the context of the encouragement of couples who are committed to the same goal of divorce-proofing their marriages. This workbook includes an easy-to-follow leader's guide.

THE 5 LOVE NEEDS OF MEN AND WOMEN
ISBN 0-8423-4239-7
Audiocassette (2 cassettes) ISBN 0-8423-3587-0

SERVING LOVE (workbook)
ISBN 0-8423-7343-8

You, too, can learn how to become your spouse's best friend with *The Five Love Needs of Men and Women* book and workbook. In this book, Gary talks to women about the deepest needs of their husbands, and Barb talks to men about the most intimate needs of their wives. You'll discover the deep yearnings of your spouse. And when you join a group studying the *Serving Love* workbook, you will learn how to understand and meet your spouse's needs within a circle of encouraging friends. They can help you find ways to meet those needs day after day, week after week. The workbook includes eight group sessions and three weekly activities. Easy-to-follow leader's guide included.

GUARD YOUR HEART
ISBN 0-8423-5732-7

GUARDING LOVE (WORKBOOK)
ISBN 0-8423-7344-6

We all need to guard our hearts and marriages. It's only in a couples small group, among like-minded friends, that you can get the solid support you need to withstand attacks on your marriage. In *Guard Your Heart,* Gary and Barb Rosberg outline the unique dangers and temptations husbands and wives face. In the *Guarding Love* workbook, Gary and Barb Rosberg give you the tools to show your small group how to hold each other accountable to guarding their marriages—no matter what the cost.

Do you know of a marriage in your church or neighborhood that is vulnerable to attack? Start a small group for that couple with the *Guarding Love* workbook as a resource. Or invite that couple to a small group that is reading and applying this book and workbook. The workbook includes eight exciting group sessions and an easy-to-follow leader's guide.

HEALING THE HURT IN YOUR MARRIAGE:
BEYOND CONFLICT TO FORGIVENESS
ISBN 1-58997-104-3
Available Spring 2004

FORGIVING LOVE (WORKBOOK)
ISBN 0-8423-7491-4
Available Spring 2004

In *Healing the Hurt in Your Marriage: Beyond Conflict to Forgiveness,* Gary and Barbara Rosberg show you how to forgive past hurt in your marriage and close the loop on unresolved conflict. Restore an honest, whole relationship with your spouse. You probably know a dozen marriages that are deteriorating because one spouse is holding a grudge or because the husband and wife have never resolved their conflict, hurt, and anger. And most marriages have past hurts that are hindering the ongoing relationship. Gary and Barbara Rosberg show you how to break free of these past hurts and experience wholeness again. The most effective way to heal wounds is within the circle of encouraging believers who understand, know, and sympathize with you in the common struggles in marriage. The *Forgiving Love* workbook is perfect for small group members who can encourage each other to resolve conflict and start the healing process. Includes eight encouraging sessions and an easy-to-follow leader's guide.

RENEWING YOUR LOVE: Devotions for Couples
ISBN 0-8423-7346-2

Have the demands of everyday life pressed in on your marriage? Has your to-do list become more important than your relationship with your spouse? Is the TV the center of your home or the love you and your spouse share? This devotional from America's Family Coaches, Gary and Barb Rosberg, will help you and your spouse focus on your marriage, your relationship, and the love of your life. Let Gary and Barb guide you through thirty days of renewal and recommitment to your marriage by reviewing forgiving love, serving love, persevering love, guarding love, celebrating love, and renewing love through the lens of Scripture, reflection, prayer, and application.

Look for a persevering love book in the future from Gary and Barbara Rosberg and Tyndale House Publishers. This book will help you weather the storms of life without losing the passion for your spouse.

Also watch for a celebrating love book from your favorite family coaches, Gary and Barb Rosberg. This book will give you creative ideas on how to keep the fire and passion alive in your marriage.

MORE RESOURCES FROM THE ROSBERGS

40 UNFORGETTABLE DATES WITH YOUR MATE
ISBN 0-8423-6106-5

When's the last time you and your spouse went on an unforgettable date? Saying "I do" certainly doesn't mean you're finished working at your marriage. Nobody ever put a tank of gas in a car and expected it to run for years. But lots of couples are running on emotional fumes of long-ago dates. Truth is, if you're not dating your spouse, your relationship is not growing. Bring the zing back into your marriage with *40 Unforgettable Dates with Your Mate,* a book that gives husbands and wives ideas on how they can meet the five love needs of their spouse. Wives, get the inside scoop on your husband. Men, discover what your wife finds irresistible. Gary and Barbara Rosberg show you how, step-by-step, in fun and creative dates.

CONNECTING WITH YOUR WIFE
ISBN 0-8423-6020-4

Want to understand your wife better? Barbara Rosberg talks directly to men about what makes women tick. She'll help you understand your wife's emotional wiring as she shows you how to communicate more effectively and connect sexually in a way that's more satisfying to your spouse. She also reveals the single best thing you can do for your marriage—and why it's so important.

Begin to divorce-proof your home, your church,
and your community today

Contact your local bookstore that sells
Christian books for all of the resources of
the Divorce-Proofing America's Marriages
campaign

or

call 888-ROSBERG (888-767-2374)

or

visit our Web site at

www.divorceproof.com.

LOVE NEEDS FOR
HUSBANDS AND WIVES

The findings here represent the categorical data that emerged from our survey of 700 couples in 8 cities. We gave each husband and each wife a list of 20 needs and asked them to rank them in order of importance.

Husbands' Needs

1. Unconditional Love and acceptance.
2. Sexual intimacy
3. Companionship
4. Encouragement and affirmation
5. Spiritual intimacy
6. Trust
7. Honesty and openness
8. Communication and emotional intimacy
9. Family relationships
10. To be desired
11. Career support
12. To provide and protect
13. Personal time
14. Understanding and empathy
15. Admiration
16. Security and stability
17. Significance
18. Romance
19. Domestic support
20. Nonsexual touch

Wives' Needs

1. Unconditional love and acceptance
2. Communication and emotional intimacy
3. Spiritual intimacy
4. Encouragement and affirmation
5. Companionship
6. Family relationships
7. Honesty and openness
8. Nonsexual touch
9. Security and stability
10. Romance
11. Trust
12. Understanding and empathy
13. Sexual intimacy
14. Personal time
15. To be desired
16. Domestic support
17. To provide and protect
18. Significance
19. Admiration
20. Career support

ABOUT THE AUTHORS

Dr. Gary and Barbara Rosberg are America's Family Coaches—equipping and encouraging America's families to live and finish life well. Having been married for nearly thirty years, Gary and Barbara have a unique message for couples. The Rosbergs have committed the next decade of their ministry to divorce-proofing America's marriages. The cornerstone book in that campaign is *Divorce-Proof Your Marriage*. Other books the Rosbergs have written together include their best-selling *The Five Love Needs of Men and Women*, as well as *Guard Your Heart, Renewing Your Love: Devotions for Couples*, and *40 Unforgettable Dates with Your Mate*.

Together Gary and Barbara host a nationally syndicated, daily radio program, *America's Family Coaches . . . LIVE!* On this live call-in program heard in cities all across the country, they coach callers on many family-related issues. The Rosbergs also host a Saturday radio program on the award-winning secular WHO Radio.

Their flagship conference, "Discover the Love of Your Life All Over Again," is bringing the Divorce-Proofing America's Marriages Campaign to cities across America. They are on the national speaking teams for FamilyLife "Weekend to Remember" marriage conferences and FamilyLife "I Still Do" arena events for couples. Gary also has spoken to thousands of men at Promise Keepers stadium events annually since 1996 and to parents and adolescents at Focus on the Family "Life on the Edge Tour" events.

Gary, who earned his Ed.D. from Drake University, has been a marriage and family counselor for twenty years. He coaches CrossTrainers, a men's Bible study and accountability group of more than six hundred men.

Barbara, who earned a B.F.A. from Drake University, has written *Connecting with Your Wife* in addition to several other books with Gary. She also speaks to women, coaching and encouraging them by emphasizing their incredible value and worth.

The Rosbergs live outside Des Moines, Iowa, and are the parents of two adult daughters: Missy, a college student studying communications; and Sarah, who lives outside Des Moines with her husband, Scott, and their son, Mason.

For more information on the
Divorce-Proofing America's Marriages
campaign, contact:

America's Family Coaches
2540 105th Street, Suite 101
Des Moines, Iowa 50322
1-888-ROSBERG
www.divorceproof.com

Tune In to *America's Family Coaches . . . LIVE!*

Listen every weekday for strong coaching on all your marriage, family, and relationship questions. On this interactive, call-in broadcast, Gary and Barbara Rosberg tackle real-life issues by coaching callers on what matters most in life—relationships. Tune in and be encouraged by America's leading family coaches.

For a listing of radio stations broadcasting
America's Family Coaches . . . LIVE!
call 1-888-ROSBERG
or
visit our Web site at www.afclive.com.